The Fourth

REBECCA WILKINSON

ISBN-10: 0980906822
ISBN-13: 978-0980906820 (Gypsy Isle Publishing)

For Kathy Staples, Champion of the Old Hay Bay Church; and the late William Lamb.

The author has taken numerous creative liberties in bringing this story to life. Though some of the events portrayed are based on actual historical fact, the story and the characters are fictional.

Cover design: Mule Kimber   www.angelheartdesign.org

CHAPTER ONE

Spring. 1794. Boston.

The dark, cramped boxing hall was filled to capacity with eager bettors from all walks of life, pushing up against one another as they jostled for a coveted spot near the front of the stage. Many still wore farmer's boots and workman's smocks, having just finished a long day of labour. Near the back of the room, Daniel Hale returned from placing his bet. His tidy brown hair was pulled back with a grey ribbon to match his frock coat, and he confidently folded his arms together, crushing his white silk cravat against his vest. His coat hung open as he glanced down and grinned at his companion, a giant of a man who sat in a rickety chair made even more fragile by his sheer weight. Tall and solid, Sean Brody was an imposing figure whether sitting or standing, and his clothes were almost completely obscured by a huge dark cloak, which made him seem all the more intimidating.

Oblivious to the excited cries of the frantic boxing fans surrounding him, Sean leaned forward and rested his dimpled chin in one hand, focused intently on reading a letter. He took his time, and when finished, he nodded in satisfaction and glanced up at Daniel.

"You've labored at that letter for days," Daniel observed, "Please tell me that you're happy with it and that we can get on with business."

"I'm off to post it now," Sean confirmed, rising to his feet, "And if you're as clever as you would have me believe, you'll leave as well. This is no place for a man with any amount of coin in his pocket, and I cannot protect you once I am gone from here."

"Oh come now, Sean!" Daniel pleaded, forced to look up at his much taller friend, "You can't go! You were the best stage boxer in all the colonies at one time! Just one good punch, and we'll be rich men!"

"That was many years ago, Daniel," Sean raised his voice so that his friend could hear him above the enthusiastic crowd, "You should know better than to expect that I would ever strike another man again."

1

"Then how can you protect me at all?" Daniel wondered.

Sean's eyes darted off to the side for just a moment and he shouted, "Left!"

Daniel dove in the suggested direction, just barely missing being clipped as an unfortunate boxer went flying past and thudded to the floor, moaning.

"Does that answer your question?" Sean called out.

Daniel recovered quickly and tugged at the bottom of his frock coat to straighten it out, then crossed his arms in front of him again and stepped back over to where Sean was preparing to make his exit. "Very well, then. If you won't box, I'll not introduce you to my sister! Her eighteenth birthday party is to be held on Saturday next in Windsor. What a shame you'll miss it."

Sean shrugged. "As far as the frolic is concerned, it's true, I'd rather not attend. Spirits and dancing should never be encouraged. However, if my appearance is the only way to meet the young lady who has stolen my heart with her...stirring letters, then so it shall be." Sean tucked the completed letter inside his jacket. "I will most certainly attend, with or without your blessing, and this correspondence informs your sister of such."

With that, he started away, but Daniel rushed after him. "Wait! Sean! These fellows aren't church folk! None will be the wiser! Just one good knockout punch and we'll ride to Vermont in a golden coach!"

Sean paused in the doorway, his burly frame blocking all light from entering the building, and slightly turned his head to reply, "My dear friend, I will need no golden coach to convince your sister to marry me." He glanced off to the side, then shouted, "Right!"

"Marry you? But you've not even met--" Daniel lunged again as a boxer hurtled past, and by the time he'd straightened up and ensured the coast was clear, Sean was gone.

*****

A young house maid hurried up the lavishly carpeted staircase of the Hale's Vermont residence, one hand outstretched to grip the gleaming mahogany banister, the other clutching a letter. When Jane Morrow reached the top of the stairs, she turned and rushed into a bed chamber showing little concern as to how such antics might be disapproved of by the mansion's residents.

Standing at the dressing mirror, Charlotte Hale swung around when her chamber door flew open, a delighted smile appearing across her pleasant face when she recognized her visitor.

"Janey!" she exclaimed, then held up the gown she'd been clutching so that her friend could see every bow and ribbon trailing down along the silky powder-blue garment. Jane threw the door shut and flopped down onto the pencil bed, feigning exhaustion. Charlotte spotted the letter and quickly dropped the gown on a nearby chair, then rushed to grab the letter from her friend's hand, tearing it open.

"You must assure me that Mr. Sean Brody's correspondence is worth my losing complete feeling in both legs," Jane teased, breathing heavily.

Charlotte smiled, but did not take her eyes from the letter until she'd read it from top to bottom. "Oh, Janey, he plans to attend the frolic with Daniel!"

Jane bolted up, her apparent fatigue having passed in light of such happy news. "How romantic, Charlotte!" Adjusting her white ruffled cap, she rose up onto her knees and lifted the bottom of her cotton work dress so that she could move closer to the edge of the bed where Charlotte had plunked down. Lowering her voice and trying to contain her excitement she suggested, "I have heard that lending to their thunderous sermons, Methodist preachers are very often the most intoxicating paramours!"

Charlotte might have blushed had such a thing come from anyone but her closest friend. Instead, she turned to Jane, a look of seriousness filling her brown eyes. "His letters would confirm such a notion, Janey. Mr. Brody's words possess an unquenched fire. To be sure, a saddlebag preacher such as he has most certainly travelled far and wide, and is no doubt worldly in many ways. And of course, in a usual situation I should definitely refuse to take up correspondence with any suitor suggested by my brother."

Charlotte rose and walked to the large window that overlooked the rear grounds of her family's sprawling estate. "Daniel is known to be a bit of a scoundrel, after all. And I suspect my dear Baptist parents will be dismayed by such a match." She slowly turned back to face her friend. "However, I am afraid that if the Reverend Sean

Brody is even one third as handsome as his penmanship and manners are elegant, then I shall never be free of my infatuation with him!"

Jane jumped up and ran to join her friend at the window, taking her hands. "You will be a princess at your birthday frolic, Charlotte, and the Reverend Sean Brody, your prince!"

*****

The festivities had been underway for two hours in the Hale family's ballroom, yet still Charlotte had not seen hide nor hair of Reverend Brody. At the urging of her father she had been persuaded to extend niceties to a smitten young man whose parents were family friends, but as she danced the Scotch reel with him, her attention was drawn to the archway leading to the servant's entrance, where Jane stood holding a tray of drinks. Charlotte glanced around the room, then back to Jane, who responded with a bewildered shrug. This confirmed that she, too, had not yet seen Daniel or the far more compelling Sean Brody.

Meanwhile across the crowded room, Sean followed close at Daniel's heels as they entered and inched through the revelers, no small undertaking for a man of Brody's size. Patience was not his strong suit either, and so the small hymn book clutched tightly at his side was perhaps the one thing that allowed him to keep a cool head under such trying circumstances.

His patience was again tested when a young blonde-haired man rushed toward him, eyes gazing off in another direction. Probably sizing up the next woman he planned to accost, Sean thought to himself, and suddenly the fellow's hand flew up and knocked the preacher's book to the floor. Kneeling down to pick it up, Sean heard the scattered whispers.

"What is he doing here?" "Who would invite such a man?"

"Please accept my apologies, sir." Sean clearly detected a hint of sarcasm in the man's voice. "I'm Charles London."

Sean accepted the handshake, but still sensed something rather unapologetic in his tone. "Of course," he said quietly, "Good evening."

As he moved on, Sean glanced back and heard the young man mutter, "Methodist monster!"

"Sean!"

Daniel was at a distance, waiting for his friend to catch up, and this was the only reason Sean thought better of confronting Charles London regarding his comment. It was a society frolic, after all. As much as he disliked such events, and as much as his Methodist beliefs frowned upon them, he was here for only one purpose. To meet the woman who would be his wife. He would allow nothing to get in the way of that.

He made his way over to join his friend just as a spirited chestnut-haired girl in a bouncy blue gown appeared out of nowhere and jumped up into Daniel's arms as he laughed and swung her around.

"Too taken with business in Boston to be fitted for proper social attire, dear brother?" the young woman queried, inspecting his riding coat and boots.

"Charlotte," Daniel replied, "I wouldn't be seen in the kinds of garments they're wearing in Boston. All ribbons and bows and such. And still that powdered hair! Far too frilly for my tastes. Besides, we've only just arrived this minute!"

"Still, you could have made an effort to--" Charlotte's wandering gaze caught Sean's eye, and Daniel quickly realized that this introduction could wait no longer.

"Sister," he offered, "May I present to you my most esteemed friend, the Reverend Sean Brody. Sean, my sister Charlotte."

Daniel gently eased Charlotte to the floor, and, smiling, she delicately lifted the sides of her billowing dress and curtsied. Jane watched, transfixed, from the archway.

Charlotte looked up into Sean's eyes. "Reverend Brody, I have greatly anticipated this meeting. The tales you have written of your travels as an itinerant preacher are no less riveting than your letters are..." she glanced sideways at Daniel before continuing carefully, "Most happily received."

Sean smiled, bowing. "It is a pleasure to finally meet you as well, Miss Hale," and he reached out and gently took hold of her gloved hand.

Charlotte's smile disappeared momentarily when she noticed his scar-covered fist, and Sean's eyes immediately filled with acknowledgement. Letting go of her hand, but never lifting his eyes from hers, he continued, "All things will be revealed to you soon enough, but in the meantime, may I be so bold as to offer you a small birthday gift?"

Charlotte lowered her eyes demurely and raised her hand to her heart as Sean proudly handed her the book he'd been carrying. "Some favourite hymns," he explained, "Daniel has told me of your love of music."

Charlotte looked pleased. "How thoughtful, Reverend Brody. And how refreshing to meet one so pious as you."

Sean nodded, then added, "Oh, but I am much more than pious, Miss Lord. I am also...determined."

Charlotte returned his confident stare. "Determination is only admirable, Reverend Brody, in one whose goals are admirable, as well."

Sean bowed slightly in agreement, then glanced over toward a group of young men who had been loitering nearby. Now they were beginning to make a little commotion, pushing and shoving one another. Young Charles London was among them.

Daniel reached to take the hymn book from Charlotte. "Sister, if I may...shall we dance?"

Charlotte finally took her eyes away from Sean. "Of course, dear brother."

"Would you mind, Reverend Brody?" Daniel asked, turning to his friend and offering the book.

"By all means, sir, by all means," Sean reciprocated, "Of course you may dance with the lady."

Daniel grinned. "I was merely asking you to hold the hymnal," he said slyly, holding the book out to Sean.

"Oh, of course, of course," Sean fumbled, though he quickly recovered. He turned and took the hand of a gob-smacked Charlotte, slowly placing her delicate fingers in Daniel's, and then urged them off toward the dance floor. As he watched them twirl about, a handsome couple approached.

"Reverend Brody, I presume?" the upper crust gentleman politely inquired.

"Yes, sir," Sean replied

The man extended a hand in greeting. "Michael Hale, and this is my wife Amelia." He turned slightly toward the queenly-looking woman at his side. She held her blonde head high, as if waiting for a crown to be placed upon it.

Sean shook Michael's hand, then nodded to Mrs. Hale, and turned back to her husband. "A pleasure, sir. Your son speaks highly of you."

"Well, I must marvel at that, Reverend," Michael almost laughed.

"I know, sir, that he admires your shrewdness in business," Sean assured him.

Michael Hale shook his head, glancing over toward his son and daughter on the dance floor. "If only Daniel could learn not to fritter his savings away at lowbred rooster fights and the like."

"A noble wish indeed," Sean nodded.

When Charlotte and Daniel returned from the dance floor, Charles London made another appearance. "Mr. Hale, may I request the honour of your daughter's company on the dance floor?"

Sean quickly interjected, "Perhaps it would be more appropriate for you to put that question to Miss Hale herself, Mr. London."

Charles' face turned to stone, and though he did not turn to Sean, he addressed him. "I wonder, Reverend Brody, do you have as little respect for your church elders as you do for Mr. Hale?"

"I respect those worthy of it, sir," Sean replied flatly.

Charles chuckled and glanced up at his rival. "Well, your appearance here makes it clear you have no respect for Miss Hale, or her family. Surely you must realize that the Methodist movement is unwelcome in most places, just as it is here among highly-educated Baptists."

"Reverend Brody is my guest, Mr. London--" Daniel attempted to intervene.

Sean held up his hand as if to let Daniel know that he could handle himself. "Mr. London," he began, "The Methodist movement, as you refer to it, does continue to grow stronger, thanks especially to young men of your regard who bring it further attention by trying to suppress it. And by all means, let me make myself perfectly clear, I am not here with sermon in hand, though there is always one in my heart."

Charles rocked from one foot to the other, agitated. "Then why, exactly, are you here, Mr. Brody?" he asked, "If not to convert the masses?"

Sean grinned and stretched his hand in Charlotte's direction. "Why of course, I am here to prove my intentions to the lovely Miss Hale, who, no doubt, desires proof of my good and worthy intentions."

Amelia Hale let out a surprised gasp.

Undeterred, Sean turned toward Charlotte's male admirers, clearing his throat. Daniel cowered a little, as if expecting the walls to fall in as Sean's voice boomed across the room, "Gentlemen, if there is one among you whose affections for Miss Hale I might challenge, then you shall let it be known here. For after this evening, I shall be the lady's only suitor."

Amelia quietly urged her husband forward to confront their daughter's would-be intended. "Reverend Brody, considering that you have only just met my daughter this night, may I suggest that your fondness for her would seem rather...impulsive."

Sean nodded, "With respect, Mr. Hale, your daughter and I have occupied ourselves with welcome correspondence for the past several months. And as for your suggestion that I have acted on impulse, it is my opinion that there are men who know not their own minds - not even their own hearts, but I am not one of them."

Sean and Charlotte exchanged a quick smile.

"What challenge could a saddlebag preacher offer?" Charles spoke up, stepping forward. "I shall face you, sir!"

Sean turned to take in his opponent, nodding agreeably when he saw that it was Charles. "Very good."

Charles chuckled, glancing around at his peers, then back to Sean. "And what shall be the challenge, sir? The recitation of the Ten Commandments? In reverse, perhaps?"

There was scattered laughter throughout the room, but all went silent when Sean proceeded to remove his frock coat. "Quite the contrary," he shook his head, "The challenge shall be one of a physical nature."

Charles looked puzzled. "Physical?"

"Surely Miss Hale's attentions are worthy of any trial?" Sean queried.

Charles glanced at Charlotte and she crossed her arms, waiting for his response.

"He's only a preacher, Charles!" someone shouted from the back of the room, and then another, "The Lord forbids him to strike another man!"

The support seemed to buoy Charles' fighting spirit. "Test me, then, Preacher," he raised his voice, removing his jacket, "For it would be a shame to see a fine young woman of Miss Hale's utility fallen into the grasp of the heathen Methodists!"

There were gasps throughout the room, and the shock upon Charlotte's face was apparent. "Utility? Really, Charles!"

Sean dropped his arms to his sides and spoke calmly, "Then take aim, good sir. For surely if I am a heathen as you say, no loving God would stand in the way of my comeuppance."

Charles glanced around the silent room, spying his childhood chums as they nodded their encouragement. He looked at Charlotte's parents, to his distinguished neighbours, and finally his eyes came to rest upon the lovely Charlotte. Turning back to Sean, he took a deep breath, raising his fist and reaching up to punch his foe square in the jaw. There were "oooh's" and "ahhh's" from the crowd, but Sean did not flinch. Charles threw another punch, then another, until finally Sean reached out and grabbed Charles at the back of his waistcoat.

Daniel eagerly grabbed a drink from a nearby server's tray and moved closer to the contest to get a better look. Charlotte gasped, watching as Charles flailed helplessly, his feet a few inches off the floor. Sean slowly lifted the young man up into the air, many of the guests covering their mouths in horror at the prospect of how this might end.

With ease, Sean carried Charles over to a small collection of lounges and chairs occupied by several matrons, spellbound as they watched the proceedings. Finding a vacant wing chair, Sean plunked Charles down into it, then turned and calmly dusted himself off. The elder women gasped, shocked to have a young man in such close proximity within their sacred circle.

Humiliated, Charles London jumped up and attempted to flee the situation, tripping over a foot stool in the process and tumbling helplessly forward. Luckily he made his recovery just before plunging headlong into a group of elderly gentlemen. He shot Sean a nasty glance before turning and quickly disappearing into the crowd.

Relieved to see that no physical harm had come to anyone, Charlotte managed a smile in Sean's direction.

"I give Baptists their due," he addressed the crowd, "They are passionate in their faith, and never yet have I known one who has converted to Methodism."

"Perhaps your fortunes are about to take a turn for the better, Reverend Brody," Charlotte suggested, smiling coyly.

CHAPTER TWO

November, 1794. Windsor.

It was the happiest day of Charlotte's life. She perched up on her tiptoes to give Sean a kiss on the cheek before turning and running off to chat excitedly with Jane. Smiling, Sean watched his new bride embrace her friend.

"May I have a word, Reverend Brody?"

It was the voice of his new father in-law, and Sean nodded with respect, "Of course, sir."

Michael Hale did not look completely unhappy at the union that had taken place, and he begrudgingly admitted, "Mrs. Hale and I congratulate you. We have looked forward to Charlotte's wedding day for some time."

"So I see," Sean observed, though he was not as easily convinced as he looked over in the direction of Charlotte's mother, who stood nearby wiping away tears. "Mrs. Hale is quite obviously…overwhelmed."

Michael glanced at his wife. "Yes, well, Charlotte is our only daughter, after all, and with all due respect, Sean, we are handing her over to the care of a preacher who boxes people about the head."

Sean leaned closer and lowered his voice. "I left that life behind upon finding my true path, Mr. Hale. And may I assure you that I have every intention of seeing to it that your daughter remains a faithful servant to God, her church, and her husband."

"What consolation that is, Reverend Brody," Michael could barely control his sarcasm, "But may I suggest that Charlotte - Mrs. Brody - is accustomed to a certain…standard of living, if you will. A standard that requires that she be settled here, in Windsor, among her society friends. I think you will agree that an itinerant life would greatly deprive both you and your new wife of certain…comforts."

Sean shook his head. "Mr. Hale, I find the greatest comfort in the service of God."

Michael tightened his fists in frustration but struggled to maintain his composure. "Reverend Brody, I would like to propose an idea that I feel would be in Charlotte's best interest, which I am sure we are each equally concerned with." When Sean did not respond, Michael continued, "I would like to offer to establish you in business – any decent business of your choice, upon the condition, of course, that you will devote yourself to it and agree to abandon your preaching duties."

Sean's eyes went wide with surprise. "I was called of God to preach, sir," he objected.

"And your church is poor," Michael countered, "Though admirable in their dedication to Methodism, your members are simply not able to provide a sufficient salary now that you have a wife and eventually children on the way."

Sean remained silent. He knew that Charlotte's father was right. She had warned him that this proposition would probably come, and they had discussed the idea at length. He understood the realities of living an itinerant life once married, and regardless of his passion for the church, he did question whether or not it was fair of him to expect Charlotte and their future children to live in lower means for the rest of their lives. But then, Charlotte had assured him that their love for one another would see them through. She would trade every comfort to be with him.

Still, Michael Hale pressed on. "Barring that possibility, I would propose that if you would at least consider serving God by taking orders in some other church, one that would not require you to lead such a...nomadic life, you and my daughter would be greatly rewarded."

A short distance away, Charlotte handed her colorful bouquet of hothouse flowers to Jane. "You must take them, Janey. You can press them in a book and save them forever. And one day when we're grey with age, we can look at them together, and remember this day."

Jane smiled. "I shall never forget this day, Charlotte. You are so beautiful!"

Charlotte turned and looked over in Sean's direction as the sound of frustrated voices grew louder.

"Oh come, now, Reverend Brody! No man, no matter how pious, is above a certain amount of greed. What is your price? A thousand pounds? More?"

Sean shook his head. "I will not take your money, Mr. Hale.

Besides, riches do not lure me. They are the devil's temptation."

"Sean is already rich," Charlotte interrupted, stepping forward to slide her arm through her husband's, "Wouldn't you agree, father?"

Michael dropped his hands to his sides, perhaps resigning himself to the realization that this was a fight he might never win. "Of course, my dear daughter," he relented, "Today, Reverend Brody surely has become the richest man in all of Vermont. Again, I congratulate you both."

With that, Michael leaned forward to take his daughter's hand and planted a soft kiss upon it, then nodded to Sean and turned to step away to comfort his distraught wife.

"He is worried that he will lose me to you," Charlotte whispered, watching her father walk away.

"Every man with a daughter bemoans this day," Sean agreed, "But the Lord will bring good fortune upon our marriage, Charlotte, and your father will soon see it."

June, 1795

To the majority of sunbathers, Sean would have appeared quite inappropriately dressed for the warm summer's day, though it was clear he was not at Mill Pond to enjoy the sunny weather. Sitting on a blanket, dressed in his black preacher's trousers and jacket, he was oblivious to the stares of fellow beachgoers as he intently studied a document in his lap. His curly dark hair danced about his ears in the breeze.

Soaked from a fresh dip in the pond, Charlotte approached, happily clutching her firm, round belly beneath her bathing gown. Sean stood up to help her gently down onto the blanket, then immediately turned back to his notes.

"Sean, really," she exclaimed, "Must you work even at the beach? With all your travelling, we have so little time together as it is."

He did not look up from his papers. "My industry will be rewarded, Charlotte, when I secure a posting in England," he reminded her. "I have only to finish reading these notes from the Bishop, and then you will have my undivided attention."

"Yes, and then we shall swim to England!" she replied,

throwing her arms out in front of her in a dramatic fashion, "Oh, the theatre we shall be able to see there! Perhaps I will become a famous actress!"

Sean shook his head. "Theatre is another of the devil's temptations, Mrs. Brody," he informed her, "And as for swimming to England, I fear I would not be able to keep up with you all the way."

Charlotte slowly lowered herself down onto her back and glanced up, squinting, toward the sun. "Perhaps we need a swimming aid for you," she said thoughtfully, "Did you know that Benjamin Franklin was a master swimmer as a young man? In fact, one of his earliest inventions was a kite which he fastened with a string to his foot. The kite pulled him through the water, and he could simply raise or lower the kite to go faster or slower!"

Sean was only half-listening, and responded in kind. "I'm afraid I would simply sink, thus dragging the kite with me, my dear," he muttered.

Charlotte was undeterred. "Someday, Sean, I shall fashion a kite that will help pull us both through troubled waters. You'll see."

Finally Sean looked up from his reading and glanced over to share a smile with his wife. "I am hoping we will not face any troubled waters, Charlotte. Already it has been mentioned that a prestigious posting may come available soon in New York."

"New York?" Charlotte exclaimed, "But why would we want to go there?"

"Every posting will bring us closer to England, and a new and better life for us and the baby," he explained.

Charlotte reached down and tenderly touched her stomach. "I think this life is perfect for the baby. We are close to family and friends."

"Your family and friends," Sean shot back.

"They are yours, too!" Charlotte protested. "How dare you think anything different, Sean!"

He took a deep breath and closed his book. "I apologize, Charlotte. Of course they are--"

"Besides, you rarely speak of your own parents," she continued.

He nodded somberly, "And with good reason."

A young boy called out to his father from the shore, "Papa! Papa!" and it took Sean back to a time he had long ago promised himself he would never again recall, refusing to beg his father for mercy, yet silently praying for it. His hands shook as they always did when his father was unhappy with him. He winced at each additional and unrelenting thwack of the birch twigs to his buttocks, each sharp slap intensifying the almost unbearable sting. His trousers pulled down to his ankles, he hoped that his mother or sister would not walk into the room and see him in such a condition; he prayed that it would be over soon, that he could lie face-down on his lumpy mattress, unmoving, so that the pain would subside at least enough that he would be able to stand up again.

Finally he heard his father step back, groaning from the effort such a thrashing had required. Sean squeezed his eyes shut, trying to keep his tears from showing, the soreness around his right eye a reminder of the thumping he'd received that afternoon in the school yard.

"Now!" his father raised his deep voice, his Irish accent unmistakable, "You'll not let them lads call ya roly-poly again without givin' them a sound clobberin' will 'ya?"

Sean shook his head and swallowed hard, "No, sir."

The next day, swearing to die before suffering such indignities ever again, he waited for his tormentors, discovering for the first time that his bare fists and angry determination could accomplish more than he'd ever imagined.

"Sean?"

Shore birds squawked from the blue sky overhead, and Sean turned, realizing that Charlotte was staring at the light bruise around his eye. She reached up toward the wound. "My poor Sean. It's still there. If you had only not happened along that dark alley at the very moment those scoundrels were scuffling, you would not be sitting here now bearing the result of a wayward blow."

Sean turned away from her touch, and she pulled back instinctively. "What is it?" she wondered.

"No need to aggravate it," he explained.

"I was merely--"

"There is no help for it, Charlotte!" he snapped, "The sooner we move past it the sooner God will allow it to heal."

Charlotte relented and looked away sourly out toward the water. "One wonders why God would allow it to happen in the first place," she mumbled.

Sean did not like to hear her questioning God, yet he could not press the conversation any further. He had not told Charlotte the full story, that he'd unexpectedly crossed paths with a handful of drunk ruffians while walking home after ministering to an unfortunate family on the other side of town. Eight children had just lost their mother as she gave birth to number nine. Afterward, Sean walked home as if in a trance, wandering almost aimlessly and in no hurry to arrive home to have to report the desperately sad story to Charlotte. The alleyway was black, but it occurred to Sean that perhaps there might be wayfarers here, sleeping in hidden squalor away from the street. Perhaps he could offer some words or guidance that might bring them to God.

The shadows approaching were not feeble and tired. Instead, they were boisterous, jumping upon one another and laughing. Until they saw Sean.

He hadn't fought back, had solidly stood his ground, his fists clenched to his sides as they threw punch after punch, laughing, amazed he was not defending himself. Sean convinced himself it had been a test. If he could defend himself without returning a blow, it meant that God was protecting him, and God did protect him. This time.

*****

Abigail Brody was born in September, and her appearance ushered in a time of great happiness in the Hale house. Out of necessity, Sean and Charlotte had lived with Michael and Amelia Hale since their wedding day, a saddlebag preacher's salary hardly being sufficient to support the newlyweds. It had not been Sean's preference, but he relented when Charlotte insisted it would have to be so, or she would not marry him at all. He had hoped that he might prove Michael Hale wrong by working tirelessly to earn the respect of the Bishop and perhaps a healthy salary increase. Alas, he discovered that hard work was rarely tireless, and the Bishop seemed to expect even harder labour when he saw how much Sean could accomplish in a short period of time.

While Sean travelled his circuit, Charlotte luxuriated in her new life as a young mother with servants to help. Frequent feedings aside, there were opportunities to leave Abigail in the capable hands of Cealy, the house maid who been Charlotte's nanny. In those moments of freedom, Charlotte liked to join Janey, arm in arm, on leisurely winter walks.

"You must be careful to not become too complacent here," Mrs. Hale warned her daughter one afternoon as they sipped tea together, "Your husband has made it clear to your father that this will not be a permanent arrangement."

Charlotte set her tea cup and saucer on the table in front of her and glanced across at her mother. "My happiness is important to Sean," she replied, "And now that we have Abigail, I cannot imagine why he would want to disrupt our lives." She paused, then added, "I am, however, aware that such things may be out of Sean's control. If we are forced to leave this house, or God forbid, to leave Windsor, I will go willingly and support my husband."

Mrs. Hale raised her tea cup to her lips with dainty fingers and sipped, then placed the cup back on the saucer and stared at her daughter with serious eyes. "If he decides to take you somewhere you do not want to go, your father and I would be happy to have you and Abigail stay here indefinitely."

Charlotte's eyes widened. "I could never leave Sean!" she insisted.

Her mother nodded. "You may feel that way now, but when faced with the prospect of introducing your daughter to a foreign life--"

Charlotte stood up, pushing her chair out behind her, "I will go anywhere that God and Sean call upon me to go!"

"You say God and Sean as if they are one and the same," Mrs. Hale quipped.

Charlotte took a deep breath, then slowly exhaled. "Imagine, Mother, how you would feel if someone were constantly speaking poorly of your husband, the man you love with all your heart. I am certain you would not tolerate such nonsense, and neither will I."

With that, she turned and swiftly left the room. Knowing her mother as well as she did, Charlotte was not surprised at her behaviour, yet she felt disappointed that her parents refused to accept Sean.

She saw very little of her husband as Abigail grew during those first many months, but through it all, Charlotte was determined to remain loyal to her Sean. This, in spite of her parents' constant judgements of him. A part of her was pleased when he delivered the news that the Bishop was sending them to New York. It meant that she would no longer need to feel torn between her love for Sean and loyalty to her parents. Even so, Charlotte knew that she would miss her family, and the comfort of Windsor.

*****

"I am home, little Abigail!" Sean called out, closing the door behind him to keep out the cold. He glanced expectantly along the small hallway and then heard his daughter's feet come running down the creaky stairs to meet him.

"Careful now my little one!" he cautioned as she jumped into his arms.

"I am not little!" she scolded, kissing him on the nose, "I will be five years old in September!"

Sean pulled her close and felt her wrap herself tightly around him. "September is many months off!" he reminded her. "Besides, you will always be little to me."

Charlotte appeared out of the small kitchen at the end of the hall, and though she did not run to him as their daughter had, Sean recognized the look of relief on her face. She was glad to have him home. She looked tired, but she smiled and reached out to him, and he gladly pulled her to him. Abigail giggled and put her arms around them both.

With each passing year Sean had hoped that there would be good news from across the sea, but no English posting had materialized. He wondered if it could be for the best. After all, it had been painful tearing Charlotte and their young daughter away from the Hale family in Windsor, so how might a move to England affect things? The coach trip to the house in Vermont took upwards of a week, and so there were few family visits back and forth.

Though the first five years had passed quickly, they had been arduous. Methodism was growing by leaps and bounds, but the membership was still made up of many of the poorest souls which could be found. Sean's salary was based on what the members could afford, and so there were many days when he did not know how his small family would survive. Still, he knew that ministering to the poor was one of the best qualities of a good Methodist preacher. That night as he lay in bed beside Charlotte, they discussed their present condition.

"We are fortunate to have only Abigail," Charlotte half-whispered, lest their daughter overhear from the next room, "For I fear we would not have food enough for even one more child." She choked back tears, and Sean carefully rolled over to face her, putting an arm across her chest to offer comfort.

"If another child comes, we will find a way," he assured her.

"How?" Charlotte challenged, "You do not know what it is like when you are away for weeks on end, Sean! You leave me with only a handful of coins and expect me to make them last until you are home again. I have been tempted to write to my father--"

"You must not!" Sean raised his voice and she silenced him immediately.

"Shush! You will wake Abigail!"

Sean let out a deep breath to calm himself before continuing, "John Wesley himself said that a rich man is not only one who has treasures of gold and silver, Charlotte. One who has food and raiment sufficient for himself and his family is rich."

"Well if John Wesley still lived, I should invite him here to dine with us on whatever small bits of food I can muster together."

Sean began to protest, "We do not suffer--"

"We are as close to suffering as I ever want to be!" Charlotte interrupted, "You are not here to see it, Sean. You are nearly always on your circuit, staying with others who feed you, while I struggle here in this city to feed our daughter!" She turned from him then, closing her eyes.

Sean pulled his arm away and rolled over onto his back, staring up at the dark wooden beams on the ceiling above them. Charlotte was right. This was no way to live. He had promised her that he would provide a good life for her and their children. He would pray to God and find a way to take care of his family.

*****

April was an unpredictable month when it came to the weather, but on this day the sun was shining as Sean approached John Street church on foot. There was still snow in the streets, though not nearly as much as there had been when he'd arrived back from the circuit in January.

He looked upward, feeling the warmth on his face as he closed his eyes. When he opened them again, he was surprised to see a familiar young man standing just outside the church door, his cheek badly bruised. Sean slowed his pace, swallowing hard, uncertain of what to expect. They'd last met on a stage he should never have set foot on, but he had prayed to God for forgiveness since then. The rewards, in spite of the sin, were great. The church had benefitted, and so had his family. Charlotte had not once questioned how his income had suddenly increased in the past months, and she seemed happy again.

Almost self-consciously, Sean glanced down at his ministerial attire, and when he looked up again, the young man stole a quick glance in his direction and then hurried away.

As he entered the church, Sean saw two men huddled together near the pulpit, speaking in hushed tones. The younger of the two, the spindly Reverend Lockwood, was motioning wildly with his hands, obviously upset. His body and limbs were lanky, red hair spraying from his head like a fountain. The elder man, Bishop Weston, finished listening before nodding and turning in Sean's direction as he approached.

"Brother Lockwood," Sean nodded.

Lockwood answered with some disdain, "Brother Brody."

"Your new hymnals arrived today, Reverend Brody," the Bishop announced.

Sean smiled approvingly. "That's grand news, Bishop. Grand news indeed. I should like to distribute them personally if you have no objection."

"Of course."

Sean began to move toward a small door that led to the church office.

Reverend Brody," Bishop Weston called out, and Sean stopped and turned back to him. "Reverend Lockwood has brought something to my attention that cannot be ignored, much as I wish it could be."

Sean rolled his eyes. "What is it this time?" he wondered, "My sermons are too thunderous? I wear my hat crooked?" He chuckled, shaking his head as he removed his hat and approached the men.

Bishop Weston shook his head. "Brother Lockwood claims to have knowledge of your involvement in recent boxing matches."

Sean glared at Lockwood.

"Where did you find the funds for the new hymnals, Reverend Brody?" the Bishop pressed, "And the repair of the organ?"

"Where does Reverend Lockwood claim to come by his knowledge of my supposed clandestine activities?" Sean clasped his hands safely out of sight behind his back, lest their slight shaking give him away.

"His suspicions were first aroused not long after you returned from your circuit in February and he saw bruising on your face," Bishop Weston paused before continuing, "I am never quick to fall under the spell of such accusations, but today he brought forward a man who confessed you recently beat him until he was bloody. His face bears the evidence still."

Sean was confused. "The man I just saw outside?" he wondered, "He was lying, Father--"

"Why would he lie, Sean?" the Bishop countered.

Sean glared at Lockwood. "You know this is not the truth!" he challenged.

"Can you prove otherwise?" Lockwood shrugged, "For we have a witness who has confessed you were his opponent in a boxing match on which men bet their wages, in some cases perhaps their life savings."

"Is it true, Sean?" Bishop Weston pressed.

It was not the whole truth, but there was enough truth to it that Sean could not deny his involvement. "We had not enough hymnals to satisfy the church," he finally confessed, "And hardly enough funds in the treasury to last us the month."

"The Lord has always provided, Sean," the Bishop reminded him sternly, "And this brings to mind what my mother used to say when--"

"Riches are the devil's temptation," Sean interrupted, "I know the saying well."

Bishop Weston managed a weak smile. "In the past you have

made me aware of your wish to take your work to the heart of Wesley's England, Sean," he said.

Sean brightened. "To devote my life to Wesley's teachings in the very place where it all began would be a humble tribute I would be proud to offer my church, Father."

"Very well," the Bishop conceded, "Then you shall go to England."

Sean narrowed his eyes, not trusting it could all be as easy as this.

"But not until you have proven to me that you have left all wickedness behind," Weston added.

Sean nodded. "Father, I shall do anything to prove myself."

There was a challenge in Bishop Weston's eyes when he said, "I believe you need to extricate yourself from your vices, Reverend Brody. If you can prove your worth by saving the church and souls of a small, remote settlement that has been lost to our work, you will be awarded a posting in London."

Sean could not mistake the faint grin that appeared on Lockwood's long, smug face. Disappointment welled up in his heart, and he wondered what he would tell Charlotte.

"Bishop, may we speak privately?"

Lockwood stood unmoving until Bishop Weston pointed away with a finger to indicate that he should take his leave. When he had gone, Sean spoke carefully, knowing he was already in a precarious position. "Father, would it make any difference if I told you that--"

Weston held up a hand to stop Sean from continuing. "You have already admitted your impropriety, Reverend Brody. There is nothing more to be discussed but your atonement."

Sean exhaled deeply, resigning himself to the fact that there was nothing to be done but move forward now.

"May I at least ask," he began, "That you do not tell Charlotte the reason for our departure?"

Bishop Weston regarded Sean thoughtfully. "She would not be happy to know what you have been up to," he surmised.

"I am ashamed," Sean admitted, "I know it was wrong, but I prayed to God and asked for forgiveness. I promised to make amends when I am able, and I will. Bishop Weston, I have a wife and daughter--"

"I will speak to Brother Lockwood and ensure it goes no further than our conversation today," Bishop Weston assured Sean, "Only you can make this right, Reverend Brody."

"Thank you, Bishop," Sean nodded, "I will not fail you."

"It is yourself you must not fail," the Bishop nodded.

CHAPTER THREE

Michael and Amelia Hale made the trek to New York to see the Brody family off to Upper Canada. They arrived a fortnight before their daughter's departure so that Charlotte in particular would have ample visiting time with her parents. Daniel brought Jane along the following week, and Sean was glad to see his wife happy to be once again among those she loved so dearly. It would not be long before they would be in the company of strangers, and there was no way to know what to expect when they arrived in their new home.

On the morning of their departure, Daniel helped Sean shove another bag into their already fully-packed wagon as Charlotte finished chatting with Jane. She squeezed her friend's hands, then turned and approached her parents with misty eyes. "Thank you for coming so far to see us off to the ends of the earth," she sniffed.

Amelia Hale managed a brave smile. "We love you, dear daughter," she said softly, opening her arms to Charlotte just as she glanced down and spied her granddaughter, "Oh, and you sweet Abigail!" The little girl rushed over and grabbed on to Amelia's hand.

Michael Hale reached over and placed a gentle hand on his wife's shoulder, the other around Charlotte. "We will always be here," he reminded his daughter, "Should you ever need us."

Charlotte stifled a sob and nodded, then turned to face her father. "But you must have faith in Sean, Papa. He is a good man who loves me."

Mr. Hale looked doubtful. "Let us hope he is much more than a good man, Charlotte, for where you are going, goodness may be something that is easily taken advantage of."

"Please, Michael," Amelia scolded, "Let us not make her more apprehensive."

Charlotte wiped her eyes with a hanky and looked off in the direction of the wagon, sad to see it was nearly filled. It would soon be time to leave.

Daniel reached up and gave one final push on a steamer trunk at the rear of the wagon, then turned back to Sean.

"The wilds of Upper Canada." He shook his head, then added,

"Though I'd wager if anyone were to make it there, you will."

"Sean smiled, "That's the first decent bet you've made in years!" he chuckled, "If you come to visit, we'll be in a settlement called Adolphustown in the Fourth Township."

"Sounds desperately remote, Sean," Daniel cringed, "Are you sure about this?"

"Don't let your sister overhear," Sean replied under his breath, "If she changes her mind now, we'll be living with your parents permanently."

Daniel nodded. "I understand, Sean. Just, know that we are here. We'll always be here for you and Charlotte."

Sean's eyes softened. "Daniel, you are my brother in-law. I am sorry to tell you that you are obligated to be here for us, like it or not."

They chuckled together until Abigail interrupted, reaching up to tug at Sean's cloak. "Papa!"

Sean squatted down to her level and smiled. "What is it, my little Abigail?" he wondered.

"Mama does not want to leave," she lamented, "I think she is sad."

Sean thought for a moment, then said, "Little Abigail, do you remember Mama telling us how she is tired of corn bread?"

"I am tired of it too, Papa!" Abigail piped up, and Sean chuckled.

"Well, I hear that the wheat is plenty where we are going, so once we are there, you can both have all the wheat bread you wish!"

"Really, Papa?" Abigail exclaimed, and she leaned forward and hugged him so tightly he almost fell backward onto the ground.

Charlotte appeared at their side, her parents trailing quietly behind. Michael Hale stepped closer, holding out a coin bag. "This may be useful, Reverend Brody," he offered, "It should be enough to give you a good start."

Sean stood and shook his head in refusal, "The Lord will provide, sir--"

But before he could give his "riches are the Devil's temptation" speech, Charlotte reached out and took the bag. "The Lord certainly does provide, my good husband," she nodded, 'Thank you, Papa."

Sean shot Charlotte a disappointed look, but he reminded himself how upset she was about leaving. "Very well then, darling. At least put it out of sight."

Charlotte nodded. "Let us be on our way, Reverend Brody," and she took Abigail's hand in hers, "I do not relish long goodbyes."

She tucked the coins into the pocket of her overcoat, then turned to face her brother. "Watch after my Janey, dear brother," she whispered, perching up on her tiptoes to hug him, "For she will need a friend now more than ever."

"So shall we all, Charlotte," he said sadly, "So shall we all."

Abigail threw her arms around Daniel's waist. "Goodbye, uncle," she said, squeezing tightly.

Now Charlotte turned to her best friend. "Oh, Janey!" she exclaimed, unable to keep her true feelings hidden a moment longer. She fell into Jane's arms, crying, and the two began to weep.

"I have asked my father to allow you to sleep in my chamber whenever you are missing me," Charlotte told her.

"But it wouldn't be proper, Charlotte!" Jane protested, "What will the others--"

"You've spent enough nights in that chamber with me over the years, Janey," Charlotte insisted, "My parents love you. You are part of the family. And you are my best friend. Now…"

"…and always." Jane finished tearfully.

"And always." Charlotte repeated.

Sean offered his hand to help his wife up onto the seat of the wagon, then lifted Abigail up beside her. Daniel moved closer to Jane, and Michael Hale stepped back, gently pulling his wife to his side, all of them watching as the wagon started away.

Charlotte was unable to bring herself to look back at them, so great was the pain of leaving. "Farewell, my dear family," she whispered sadly.

"Never mind, dear mother," Abigail soothed, clasping her mother's hand, "Papa says we won't have to eat any corn bread in Canada!"

*****

The journey took many days, and though Sean insisted they could seek shelter in the homes of Methodist followers along the way, Charlotte was equally as stubborn, demanding they stay at inns whenever possible. Proper lodgings were scarce, but Sean was at least able to use his powers of persuasion to convince Abigail that they had embarked upon an exciting adventure. If only her mother could be as easily swayed.

On the final day of their travels, dark clouds moved in overhead, and rain fell for most of the afternoon. Thick forest surrounded them, and in spite of the pouring rain, they found themselves constantly slapping at mosquitoes. Charlotte glanced down at her dress, dirtied and torn from the unavoidable branches that reached out and pulled at her along the way. She lifted a hand to her head and was not surprised to discover that her hair had fallen into a dreadful state, her hat perched precariously upon the disastrous mess. "I have never seen raindrops so huge! Honestly, Sean, won't we soon be there?" she fretted.

"It would be easier on horseback," he hinted

Charlotte considered this. "But that would mean…"

"Leaving the wagon behind, yes," he replied matter-of-factly.

"Could we come back for it later?" she ventured.

Sean cracked the reins, urging the horses to pull harder.

"Perhaps," he replied, "Although in truth it may not be here later. This is a desperate place, Mrs. Brody."

"When will we be there, Mama?" Abigail whined, leaning her head on Charlotte's shoulder, "I don't like this adventure any longer."

A mile or so from their destination, the wagon became mired in the muddy, nearly impassable road, and suddenly Charlotte didn't care if they lost everything. She only longed to be out of the rain, nestled in front of a glowing fire, a china tea cup in her hand. They were as far from civilization as she could imagine. She couldn't believe that anyone out here would care if she were forced to wear the same dress forever if the steamer trunk were stolen. She would make more clothes, buy clothes with the money her father had given them. She didn't care. Right now, she only wanted to be warm and dry.

Sean seemed pleased when she finally pleaded to abandon the wagon, and he went about saddling up the two horses for riding.

The rain had stopped by the time they reached the settlement, but there was a sea of mud everywhere as Sean and Charlotte dismounted, weary and tattered, near a small cabin.

Sean pulled an almost-limp Abigail down from the saddle she'd been sharing with him, and Charlotte went to her, wrapping her arms around her daughter for comfort.

A blonde-haired man opened the cabin door and stepped out, an almost suspicious look upon his face. His face was red and weathered, and he did not appear to be at all excited at the prospect of visitors.

"Could you direct me to the cabin of Mr. Hollister?" Sean asked politely.

"I suspect you're the Brody family," the man nodded, crossing his arms in front of him and glancing over at Charlotte and Abigail.

"I am the Reverend Sean Brody, and this is Mrs. Brody," Sean extended a hand in the direction of Charlotte, who dropped her head slightly, no doubt preferring to have as little attention as possible directed toward her in her present state.

"There's no need for pleasantries, Mr. Brody," the settler cut in, "I'm an honest man, so I'll tell you plainly that we haven't seen the same saddlebag preacher's face in this settlement more than twice. They're few and far between, and there hasn't been one here in a few years. So I don't imagine there'd be much sense in my taking the time to get comfortable with you, either."

Charlotte was immediately offended. "Nor do we see any merit in wasting our time standing here chatting with you in the rain," she shot back, waving her arms in the air at the cloud of mosquitos above her head, "We are to stay with the Hollisters until we are settled, so if you could please direct us toward--"

"I'm Willem Hollister," the man interrupted, "So you need go no further."

Sean frowned, "The American Conference has promised a generous stipend in return for your hospitality, sir, so I do expect you have made arrangements for our arrival."

"That stipend is the only reason I agreed to their request," Hollister admitted, then turned back toward the cabin and stepped inside, leaving the door open behind him.

Sean and Charlotte glanced at one another, unsure of whether or not they should proceed.

"Come in and close the door!" Willem yelled from inside.

Charlotte took Abigail's hand and slowly pulled her toward the cabin, motioning for Sean to go ahead of them. Just before entering, he paused and looked up at the building as if to speak to it, "Peace be to this house," he proclaimed.

Stepping inside a large kitchen, they were met with a sudden chorus of enthusiastic young voices, which were hushed when it became apparent there were visitors. A teenage boy, almost a man, sat in a corner holding a book in his hand as he read to a young brother sitting at his feet. Three young girls quickly ran to one another and joined hands, trying to contain their excitement as they gazed at Abigail with curious eyes.

Willem's wife was standing back from the fire, a baby boy slung over her shoulder. She watched an older teenage girl tending a pot over the hearth. The young woman turned to curiously inspect the trio, and her mother noticed this, tapping her shoulder and handing her daughter a kitchen cloth, urging her to get back to her tasks. "Keep an eye, Susannah," she encouraged, before smoothing her skirts with her free hand and turning to offer a smile to greet her guests.

"Liza, this is Reverend and Mrs. Brody," Willem offered. Charlotte was pleased and not a little surprised that a man who seemed so sullen only moments ago could suddenly show a polite side. Perhaps there was hope for him yet.

A young girl pulled away from the line and grabbed protectively onto her mother's leg. "Her name's Eliza, not Liza, if you please!" the girl announced, and Abigail stepped timidly behind her mother.

"Emma!" Eliza scolded, touching her young one's head. "I am sorry. We don't often see new people. Welcome," she smiled.

Charlotte nodded. "Thank you. I must apologize for our state. We have been travelling all day and--"

"Of course," Eliza interjected, "I'm sure that you and the Reverend would like to rest." She turned slightly to look at the girls behind her, "Phoebe...please show the Reverend and Mrs. Brody to their new home." She looked down at Abigail, peeking out from behind her mother's skirts, "My Emma looks to be close to your age," she nodded, "She's nearly six."

"I will be five in September," Abigail piped up.

"Oh, well you are nearly a young lady, then!" Eliza smiled, "Perhaps I should send Emma instead--"

"Yes please, Mama!" Emma tugged at her mother's dress, grinned happily at Abigail, and then skipped to the door, pulling it open and waving a hand in the air to invite them to follow her. She led them to a small wooden shanty not far from the Hollister's cabin, but as they drew near, Sean paused and looked across the way at a larger building. The signboard above the doorway read, "TAVERN".

"That's Papa's place!" Emma shouted excitedly, "The first tavern in Adolphustown!"

"And hopefully the last," Sean muttered.

Charlotte was more interested in finally being able to tuck Abigail into a bed to pay too much attention to the concerns of her husband. She eagerly followed Emma inside the shanty, her breath leaving her momentarily when she saw what awaited them.

There was a small, lumpy mattress on the floor in one corner. A dilapidated chair sat beneath the tiny, lone window, over which hung an over-sized piece of cloth in lieu of an appropriate curtain. There was a small kitchen area, an old bake kettle near the hearth, and a small table fashioned from a tree trunk.

"This is where Papa lived with his first family before he married Mama," Emma explained, glancing around the room as if it were a wonderland.

"I see," Charlotte smiled politely, "And where is his first family now?"

"His wife died," Emma nodded matter -of-factly, "Cornelia is married and away, but Bram and Susannah still live with us because they haven't found people to marry yet!" she giggled, glancing at Abigail.

Abigail smirked and covered her mouth to stifle a chuckle.

"It's so tiny!" Charlotte remarked, "However could an entire family squeeze into such a small place?"

"Papa and his family lived in a tent before this," Emma explained, "They were real happy when this finally got built."

Charlotte was humbled. "Of course," she smiled, "Of course they were."

Sean gently ushered Emma over toward the open door. The sound of evening bird calls rang out from the nearby woods. "We shall be as happy here as your father's family was, young lady," he assured her, "Thank you. Please tell your parents we will rest now."

Emma nodded and ran excitedly out the door, leaving the fascinating newcomers to settle in.

Charlotte moved to the small window and lifted the curtain a little to peer out. "Now that we're here, perhaps Mr. Hollister might rally a few of the men to help pull the wagon out," she suggested.

Sean removed his hat. "Now that we're here," he repeated, "Perhaps we should take the opportunity to rest. It will be dark soon. Besides, is there really anything in the wagon that we will need tonight?"

Charlotte gasped. "If you consider cooking pots to be unnecessary, then perhaps you'll agree that meals are unnecessary, as well, Reverend Brody!"

Sean let out a frustrated sigh and pulled his hat on again, turning without a word and stomping back out through the tiny door just as the rain started up again.

"Sean!" Charlotte called out after him, "Sean!" But he was in no mood to listen to her.

Charlotte stood in the doorway and watched him slog away in the mud toward his horse, mounting up and galloping off onto the path from whence they'd come. Surely he wasn't planning to try to retrieve the wagon on his own?

"Mama!" Abigail called out, and Charlotte turned to see her little girl lying exhausted on the mattress, "I'm hungry!"

*****

The wagon had sunk even deeper into the mud by the time Sean got back to it. He chided himself for being too stubborn to ask for help, yet at the same time he hardly felt justified in dragging strangers out in the middle of a downpour to help him with such a task. Perhaps if he could manage this himself, it would show Charlotte that he had been paying attention to her concerns. She was a good wife and mother. He wanted her to feel as

31

comfortable as possible in their new home. The Lord knew they already faced a great challenge, having landed in this place that might test their faith, not just in God, but in one another as well.

He put his hands on his hips and let out a great sigh, wondering where to begin. Perhaps if he could somehow move away some of the mud under the wheels—

A branch snapped loudly nearby and Sean swung around in the direction of the sound. A squirrel bounded rapidly up the weathered bark of an old oak tree, and Sean squinted in the dusky light, but could not see any other sign of life. The rain began to pour harder, and he pulled down the brim of his black preacher's hat to better cover his face.

He glanced up past the tops of the trees, the dark clouds passing quickly overhead. It looked like there was a path leading into the forest that might be a quicker route back to the shanty, but Sean knew the woods would soon be difficult to find his way out of, even with a blazed path to guide him, for the axe marks would not be visible once darkness fell. He hitched up his horse and tried to pull the wagon out, but it would not budge, even if there were two horses, he thought to himself.

As his boots sunk slowly into the mud, he struggled to pull up one foot and then the other, the sludge filling in around each foot, threatening to pull him in as deep as the wagon. Finally he managed to free himself, though he almost lost his boots, his foot coming completely out of one as it lodged itself in the mire. It was no use. As much as he wanted to make their first night easier, he finally gave up and went home to Charlotte. He walked through the door, his coat drenched from the downpour, and mud oozing down his boots.

She was sitting at the table wringing her hands, and when she stood up and went to him, a look of concern crossed her face. "You went to the wagon alone, didn't you?" she asked him.

"We'll have to wait until the rain lets up," he informed her, sliding his hat from his head. He glanced over and saw Abigail fast asleep on the mattress.

"She was famished. The Hollisters gave us supper," Charlotte told him, "Eliza said she would hold a plate for you." She reached up and brushed back his wet hair. Sean leaned down, encouraged, and touched his lips to hers. At first she seemed to respond the way he'd hoped she would, but then without warning, Charlotte abruptly pulled away and turned from him. "Abigail could wake up, Mr. Brody," she reminded him, attempting to tuck her already-frazzled hair into place. "You should eat," she suggested.

Sean stepped back, nodding, and took a deep breath. He understood all too well that once again, Charlotte was making excuses. She knew as well as he did that Abigail slept like a log and would most certainly welcome a good night's rest after the long journey. The child would not wake if a cannon ball came crashing through the tiny shanty.

"I've suddenly not much of an appetite," he announced. "You share the mattress with Abigail. I will find a bench at the church." Returning his hat to his head, he turned and left, this time slamming the door behind him.

She went after him, "You do not know where the church is, Sean! It is almost dark!" she called out.

"I will find it," he yelled over his shoulder.

Charlotte raised a hand to her mouth, closed her eyes, and scolded herself. She did not want to push him away, especially on a night like this. They were in a strange place, and there could be dangers all around them. She pushed the door shut and fell against it. What had they done by coming here? How could they live in such a place, or raise Little Abigail here? Oh, how she missed her mother. How she missed Janey. The distance she had felt from Sean during most of the journey had been of great concern, and tonight, when she needed him the most, she felt the rift growing even deeper. How could he leave his wife and young daughter to their own defenses? What frightening circumstances awaited them in this horrible wilderness?

Charlotte plopped down at the makeshift table, dropped her face in her hands, and began to cry.

*****

Outside the cabin, Sean paused and took a deep breath. The rain had stopped. It had been a long, difficult trip. Perhaps both he and Charlotte would feel better tomorrow after a good night's rest.

He heard a knock and looked over to see a man at the Hollister cabin. Sean remained quiet in the shadows and watched. The man spit out his tobacco as Willem opened the door.

"See 'ya for a bit, Willem?"

Willem hesitated, and Eliza appeared in the doorway beside him, concern on her face. "Is anything the matter, Sheriff Cain?" she queried.

Cain tipped his hat to Eliza. "You're looking fair this evening, Mrs. Hollister," he smiled.

Willem reached back and pushed his wife safely behind him. "Let me get my hat," he suggested.

"Best be hasty about it," Cain said impatiently. He turned to glance around the settlement and Sean instinctively drew back around the corner of the shanty so as not to be seen.

After a moment the door opened again and Willem stepped outside. Sean watched them disappear onto a footpath that led into the woods. Presently he heard them arguing, and out of curiosity he began to move toward the sound of their voices. He picked up his pace when he heard a punch, but before he reached the path he saw Sheriff Cain stumble out into the clearing, holding his head.

Willem appeared out of the woods and was about to strike the Sheriff again when Sean intervened and pulled him away from the slightly smaller man. Cain recovered quickly, reaching down to his boot and producing a knife, which he waved in the air toward Willem.

"You might tell me now if you can't make good on the terms, Hollister," he warned, "Otherwise you'll be needing to keep a more watchful eye on those pretty little daughters of yours--"

Willem tried to rush at Sheriff Cain again, but Sean grabbed him and held him back.

Still holding the knife out in front of him, Cain began to back away. "You might want to thank this fella Hollister," he suggested, "He just saved your wife from becoming a widow by morning."

Cain turned, quickly disappearing into the night, and Willem pulled away from Sean to inspect his bloody fist.

"You'll need that attended to," Sean insisted.

"Lucky for him it was a tree that I hit the second time and not him," Willem admitted.

"I have some experience with injuries of this nature," Sean replied, undeterred, "Might I help you--"

"It's not your business, Reverend," Willem insisted, "You'd

best stay out of it."

He turned then and made his way back to his cabin.

CHAPTER FOUR

Charlotte was awakened on their first morning in Adolphustown when Abigail, wearing only her shift, pushed open the door and allowed the sun to flood into their little shanty. The meager fire she had managed to start last evening had long since extinguished itself, and there was no sign of Sean.

"Please close it, darling," Charlotte urged, shivering from the chill, "We must get dressed."

Abigail closed the door as Charlotte rolled off the mattress and slowly stood up, every muscle in her body sore. She was worried about Sean. Had he found the church? Even then, what kind of sleep would he have had on a bench? Then, glancing around their sad little room, she realized there would not have been much comfort for him here either.

She went to the rickety chair near the cold hearth over which she'd hung her travelling dress and Abigail's as well. She'd hoped they might dry sufficiently by morning, and though they were still damp, they would have to do. "We will walk a sunny path today to dry out," she smiled at Abigail as they dressed.

They made their way along the worn footpath that Charlotte assumed must certainly lead to the church, as it appeared that walking in the other direction would take them directly into the forest. The Hollister's cabin seemed to be at the farthest edge of the back of the settlement, looking out over the section of the Bay of Quinte called "Hay Bay" by the locals. The main road they'd travelled on to reach the front part of the settlement had seemed far more inhabited, and she wished they could have found lodging there. However, Sean wanted to be nearer to the meeting house, and with the Conference having already made arrangements for their accommodation with grumpy Mr. Hollister, Charlotte had little choice in the matter.

"When will we eat, Mama?" Abigail wondered, pulling down on Charlotte's hand.

"We must find your father first," Charlotte insisted, "We will not starve."

"I feel like I may indeed starve," Abigail complained.

Charlotte smiled, glancing down at her daughter. When she

looked up again, she realized that curious eyes watched them from tiny windows and makeshift porches along the way. She'd done her best to tidy both herself and Abigail, but she was relieved just the same when they finally saw the small church come in to view not far ahead near the shore of the bay.

On the ground near the door she spotted a large stick of wood with nails jutting out of it, and she directed Abigail to make a wide berth around it. From outside, the meeting house looked as plain and unimpressive as any; a simple frame church with mostly boarded-up windows on two levels all around, and comfortably situated on the banks of the quiet bay. The sparse patch of land on which it had been erected was devoid of trees, though as she looked toward the gentle sloping grass that led down to the water's edge, Charlotte saw lush green willows, their lovely branches drooping down into the water.

She carefully pulled open the door, and Abigail bounded in ahead of her.

Sean was sitting at a small desk near the front of the church, books open in front of him. Only one shutter was open, allowing a stream of light to shine on his reading.

Charlotte wasn't certain what to expect. Would he want to see her?

Abigail ran to him and he stood up with a weary smile to hug her.

"I will open the other shutters," Charlotte offered.

"Wait, Mrs. Brody," and she stopped, turning back to him as he approached. Abigail scurried up the back steps to inspect the small balcony area and watched from above as her parents embraced.

"I am sorry for last night, Sean," Charlotte whispered, thankful to be in his arms again.

"Today is a new day," he told her, and he kissed her forehead, "Let us rejoice."

Charlotte felt relief wash over her, determined to ensure her family would always be happy, even in the most trying of circumstances.

As they left the church, she pointed to the large piece of wood she'd seen on the way in.

"It was nailed across the door," Sean told her, "Someone doesn't want the Methodists of Adolphustown to attend their own meeting house."

They wandered back along the path, passing Mr. Hanley's general store, and Charlotte felt excited at the prospect of using some of her father's coins to stock their tiny kitchen with cooking supplies. "Sean," she ventured, "Now that the rain has stopped, perhaps the wagon can be moved."

"I will ride back out toward the front and have a look at it today," Sean nodded.

They arrived at the Hollister's cabin in time for breakfast. "There's enough for everyone!" Eliza chirped as children scurried around her skirts. "You can help us finish off the salt pork," she added, handing Charlotte an apron.

Sean and Willem stepped outside, and Charlotte was hopeful they'd be discussing retrieval of the wagon.

"We found you a bed," Eliza grinned, "The Van Horns had an extra with a pigeon feather mattress. They heard the new preacher slept on a bench last night and Walter was at the door first thing this morning."

"Oh Eliza, that's wonderful!" Charlotte exclaimed, her heart filling with hope, "I am so looking forward to Sean's first service this Sunday." She set a stack of plates on the table and glanced out the window along the path toward the church, "That meeting house needs a good cleaning," she said absently.

"You may not have to worry about that," Eliza shooed one of the children away from the hearth, where the eggs were frying.

"Whatever do you mean?" Charlotte wondered.

Eliza paused. "We've been on our own in this place since first we landed on its shores, Charlotte. We love God, and we know he loves us, but few Methodist preachers hazard to travel this far, and they never stay for long. As it is, any young couples wanting to be married are required to travel all the way to Bath to see the Anglican minister, Josiah Hamm. He's the only one available most times, and you'd best be at his church by noon, else he closes his pocket watch at exactly that time and leaves."

Charlotte thought back to her own wedding to Sean. It had been the most wonderful day of her life. There had been so many plans; a dress had to be made especially for the occasion. Neighbours came from many miles to be part of such a special event. "Is there at the very least a party in honour of the bride and groom when they return to the settlement?"

Eliza shook her head and reached for a kitchen cloth, leaning forward to pull the pan of eggs away from the fire.

"These folks are just trying to keep their families alive, Charlotte," she explained, "You have only to look around the settlement to know that. Worshipping God has never been more of a challenge than it is here, especially with Judge Franklin Wycherley putting the fear of worship into everyone."

"Why would a judge discourage worship?" Charlotte asked.

"Your husband will find out soon enough," Eliza answered, then swung around and addressed the children, "Call your father and Reverend Brody!" she instructed, "Breakfast is ready!"

There was quite a ruckus as the Hollisters settled down to eat. The bench seats provided just enough sitting room for the large family, so extra chairs had to be found and dragged nosily to the table to accommodate company.

Sean furrowed his brow and stared across the table when young Zedekiah, just three, eagerly picked up his fork and began to devour his eggs. Eliza was the next to notice, and she reached over and took the fork from her son mid-swallow. "There is something we need to do first, Zedekiah." She glanced over at Sean. "Reverend Brody, perhaps you would honour us by saying grace before the meal?"

Sean smiled and seemed complimented to have been asked, but then caught Charlotte staring at him from across the table. "I speak too much already," he grinned, reading his wife's thoughts, "I would be pleased to allow Mr. Hollister the honour."

Silence fell over the table. The Hollister children dropped their heads, and Eliza shuffled nervously in her chair.

"Perhaps," she offered, "I could say--"

"No, Eliza," Willem jumped in, "I will do it."

Sean and Charlotte reached across the table and took one another's hands, and Abigail placed her tiny fingers on theirs.

Willem paused, taking a deep breath. "It's been some time since I've said grace," he admitted quietly.

"But Father," the sensible Phoebe piped up, "You've never said--"

"Shhhhh!" Susanna quieted her younger sister with a tap on the hand.

Willem exhaled loudly and finally mumbled, "Now...I lay me...down to sleep."

Silence followed. Abigail stifled a giggle and Charlotte squeezed her hand to quiet her, then opened her eyes to glance across at her bewildered husband.

"Amen," Sean finished loudly, and he looked up at Willem, who nodded and repeated, "Amen."

"Amen!" the children chimed in eagerly.

"Can we eat now?" Zedekiah wondered impatiently, and his question was met with hearty laughter.

*****

It didn't take long for Charlotte to discover that Eliza's prediction had been accurate. She and Abigail had been visiting settlers' homes all morning, and those few who had allowed her inside seemed more curious to learn more about her than they were interested in hearing about Sean's mission. She could see they would need some persuasion to return to the church. Regardless, she carried on and rapped upon another cabin door, attempting to arrange her disheveled hair and smooth the wrinkles from her worn dress. She reached down and took Abigail's hand, smiling.

A handsome woman opened the door. Her golden hair, pulled back, complimented her fair complexion and blue eyes, though she would have looked far prettier if she were to offer a smile, Charlotte thought.

"Good day, Madam, I am Mrs. Sean Brody."

"Are ya' now?" the woman looked her up and down with a discerning eye.

"My husband is the new Methodist preacher, the Superintendent of the Bay of Quinte circuit," Charlotte continued, undeterred, "And I'm here to inform you of the service planned for Sunday next."

"Where are you from, then, Mrs. Brody?" the woman asked.

"Windsor," Charlotte answered, then added, "Vermont."

The woman rolled her eyes. "I'm well aware that Windsor is located in Vermont, Mrs. Brody. My husband was a soldier of the King's Loyal Rangers, and though it was New York we were driven from, we are quite familiar with the colonies."

Charlotte had often thought of the poor Loyalists. So many had lost their homes and possessions during the war. "I...I am sorry," she stuttered.

"You've no need to be sorry, Mrs. Brody," the woman reassured, waving a hand in the air, "But don't expect my family to fall at your feet because you wear fancy hats and dresses, or because your luck fell on the side of the victors."

Charlotte marvelled that anyone could refer to the dress she was presently wearing as fancy. "But Madam, I assure you, I..."

"You're a far cry from Windsor now, Mrs. Brody. You'd do well to remember that," and the door slammed shut.

She shouldn't have been shocked, though Charlotte was astonished by the rudeness she had witnessed all morning. The people of Adolphustown seemed eager to turn her away, but she needed to fill that church on Sunday. Otherwise, what was the point of all that she and Sean had gone through to get here?

"Don't the people like us here, Mama?" Abigail wondered as they continued on.

"They don't know us yet," Charlotte reminded her daughter, "Once they come to know us, and especially you, Little Abigail, they will be very happy we came to Adolphustown."

Charlotte took a deep breath, filling her lungs with determination, and confidently approached the next cabin. This time it was Abigail who reached out and knocked, and Charlotte straightened up, convinced that this time she would be met with friendship and good fellowship.

The young woman who opened the door was bouncing a crying baby boy on her hip. Dark hair fell in untended curls around her face. Her apron was torn and dirty. Young children wailed somewhere behind her in the cramped, untidy surroundings.

"Hello, I am pleased to make your acquaintance," Charlotte began, "I am Mrs. Sean Brody--"

"The new preacher's wife," the woman interrupted, raising her voice to be heard above the sound of the screeching children.

"Yes!" Charlotte replied jubilantly, "And I have come to introduce myself to you, and to invite you--"

"Charity!" the woman screamed out over her shoulder, "Tend to your brothers!"

She turned back to Charlotte, still distracted, as the babies wailed louder, and Abigail cupped her hands over her ears.

"As I was saying," Charlotte continued, undeterred, "I have come to invite you and your lovely family to my husband's inaugural service at the Methodist church on Sunday next."

"Charity!" the woman screamed, "What did I tell you?"

Charlotte jumped. "Perhaps I'll come at another time," she suggested.

"No need, Mrs. Brody," the woman informed her, "We won't be at your church. There are more pressing things here at home."

"Oh, but I must implore you to reconsider--"

"I wouldn't expect the likes of you to understand," the woman snorted, "Good day, Mrs. Brody. Charity!" she shouted again as she slammed the door.

If Charlotte hadn't felt Abigail pulling at her arm, she might have stopped at that moment. She felt like closing her eyes and letting her legs give out from under her. Perhaps then Sean would see that it was time to go back to Vermont. Instead, they trudged along the worn path, stopping at every cabin and shanty along the way, though if anyone came to the door at all, an unwelcome greeting was usually received. After the last door was closed to her, she went to the only place where she thought she might feel some comfort.

Eliza was at the church. She'd opened the windows to let the air inside, and there was a nice breeze blowing in from the bay. Abigail ran to Emma and gave her a hug, and both girls skipped happily outside to play.

"Bless you, Eliza," Charlotte exclaimed, grateful to see a friendly face.

"Willem would not be happy to know I am here, but it is such a beautiful day," Eliza replied, "I noticed on my stroll with Emma that the door is no longer boarded up, and I couldn't resist coming in. I love these windows!" she finished, glancing around the church.

"After today I much prefer windows to doors," Charlotte lamented as they moved to sit in a pew.

"What has happened?" Eliza asked.

"You were right, Eliza. I was turned away at every door today. If not by Presbyterians, by Quakers, or by people who simply have no interest in attending church at all."

"If it brings you any comfort," Eliza smiled, "I saw Reverend Brody return with saddlebags filled with things from the wagon. It didn't look like anything large, of course, but perhaps enough to make it feel a little more like home for you here."

Charlotte nodded, her eyes misting over. "This may be a hard place to call home," she admitted.

Eliza nodded with understanding. "These are good people, Charlotte. And many are Methodists - the same Methodists who funded the building of this church. In fact, Willem supplied one of the largest donations."

"But why have so many fallen away from their faith?" Charlotte challenged.

"People have been frightened away by threats from Judge Wycherley. But perhaps things will change when people know that you and Reverend Brody intend to stay on," Eliza suggested.

Charlotte dropped her head a little. "They look at me with such contempt."

Eliza put her arm around Charlotte and pulled her closer. "Their hearts will warm to you. You must not give up, Charlotte."

*****

That night, Charlotte lay down on the bed given to them by the Van Horn family, and gratefully pulled the covers up around herself. She rolled over to glance in the direction of the mattress, and saw that Abigail was fast asleep.

"She must have had a long day," Sean observed, pulling off his trousers.

"We both did," Charlotte remarked, rolling over to face the wall. "Thank you for bringing a few things from the wagon. Can you fetch our table and chairs tomorrow?"

"It is now deep in hardened mud," Sean acknowledged, "But I will try to get it out on my way back from Kingston."

"Kingston!" Charlotte repeated, "But we only just arrived here, Sean!"

"I must meet brother Ezra Beckett," Sean explained, "He is familiar with this settlement. He may be able to offer some guidance."

He slipped under the threadbare blanket and pressed his body against hers, but Charlotte was having none of it. Exhausted after such a long day, she wanted nothing more than to close her eyes and drift off into a dream that would take her anywhere but Adolphustown. She knew that Sean had worked hard all day as well, carting things back and forth from the wagon on horseback. They now had some clothes and tins of food, for which she was grateful, but she knew there was so much more simply sitting there at the mercy of this wild, untended settlement.

She felt Sean tug the blanket down and she fought in vain to keep him from doing so. She was still turned away from him but knew what he was after nonetheless.

"You are still in your day dress!" he exclaimed, almost laughing as he ran his hands along her back, and she was irritated all the more.

"I have no night dress with me, Sean," then paused before adding, "You brought only two dresses of mine from the wagon."

"But surely you can remove this and sleep in your underthings!" he persisted.

"The nights are still cool here," she replied, trying to keep her voice calm, "I would most certainly risk turning to ice, Sean."

He was silent for a moment before answering, "I have the distinct feeling we are facing a frosty night ahead in any case, Mrs. Brody."

Charlotte was afraid she would explode if she allowed herself to respond to such a ridiculous comment, and so she simply tucked her hands up under her head and closed her eyes.

He tossed and turned for a few minutes, and then she was aware that Sean moved away from her as he rolled over and stood up. She hoped he might only be getting up to read by lamp light, but then she heard him quickly dress and quietly shut the door as he left. She could not resist jumping up and hurrying to the window to carefully peer out to see where he might be wandering off to, but darkness had set in, and he quickly vanished into it.

*****

Sean breathed in the fresh spring air and fought to quell his passion. He was accustomed to Charlotte pushing him away. It had been happening more frequently as time went on, but still she was a good wife, faithful and dedicated to their marriage. He knew she could not fully appreciate why he had dragged her and Abigail to this unknown land, so far from her family and friends. He had been forced to explain to her more than once that if he could be successful in his Adolphustown posting, they might soon be on their way to England, but lately he was beginning to wonder if that would be the best thing for his family after all. As much as it would plant him in the heart of the beginnings of Methodism, it would take Charlotte even farther away from those she loved, and he was beginning to wonder if perhaps his love alone was not enough for her.

*****

Willem Hollister saw movement outside in the darkness, then squinted and tried to get a better look through the small window near his kitchen table. It only took a moment for him to recognize the tall, imposing figure that was making his way along the path that led down toward the shore of the bay. "Those Brodys are a restless lot," he commented to Eliza, who sat nearby patching clothes, "If it's not the wife out knocking on doors trying to convert everyone, it's him wandering in the dark looking for someone to preach to."

Eliza smiled, not looking up from her work, "They're good folk. We should give them a chance, Willem. Especially her, poor soul. You remember what it's like to have to leave everything behind and start from nothing. She's just learning that now for the first time. And I don't imagine the preacher is making things any easier for her, leaving that wagon where it is all this time."

Sean had almost reached the shore when he heard splashing, and he looked out, scanning the calm waters. What manner of fish could make such a commotion? He had heard that the carp were monstrous in this bay, but as he watched, moving closer now, he realized that it was a person thrashing about, and no sea monster.

She came more clearly into view as she swam toward the shore, and Sean began to back away, uncertain of the circumstances. He thought it might be best to turn and hurry off, lest she be put off by the presence of a stranger, but by now she would have seen him, and besides, every citizen he met could account for another space filled in one of the empty benches at the church. Had he known that she had been swimming completely naked, he would most certainly have left the scene forthwith, but by the time she stood up in the knee-high water in the moonlight, all was revealed, and it would have been too late to pretend he hadn't seen her. Indeed, how could any man not have noticed her? Her fair, slender face was framed with long, golden hair that hung down, wet, along her shoulders, just covering her ample chest. She glanced up at him, and he quickly turned away, embarrassed that his eyes had lingered too long.

"Oh!" she exclaimed, alarmed when she finally spotted him, and he heard her scurry for cover, "I didn't know you were there!"

Sean found himself fumbling for something to say. He could not bring himself to turn to face her. It had already been a mistake to stay as long as he had, and yet, hurrying off might lead her to think he felt he had done something wrong.

"You can turn around now," she reassured him, "I am sorry. I wasn't expecting company."

Taking a deep breath, he slowly turned in her direction. He was relieved to see that she had slipped into a long shift, though she pulled the garment more tightly around her waist as she stepped closer, accentuating the outline of her curves.

"You're the new preacher," she smiled, reaching up to squeeze some water from her hair.

"Sean Brody," he nodded, relieved he was finally able to speak. It was the first time in recent memory that he had found himself without something to say.

"Well, Sean Brody, welcome to Adolphustown. I'm Caroline. You'll find me here most nights the minute the ice clears off the bay." She glanced up toward the quiet settlement. "The hours can drag awful slow in this place."

Her forthrightness did not surprise him. Sean had travelled through many communities far more uncivilized than Adolphustown.

"Who's down there?"

Sean stiffened up when he heard the familiar voice.

"Curse that man," Caroline muttered, half to herself, "He'd find me if I were two townships away."

Sean turned to look as Sheriff Cain stepped into view.

"I shoulda' known," he rolled his eyes, not attempting to hide his disdain, "Tryin' to lure him in already, are 'ya Caroline?"

Sean didn't want there to be any misunderstandings. "I was simply out for a walk, Sheriff," he jumped in, "And this young lady was--"

"Oh, I know what she was doin'," Cain cut in, moving toward Caroline, "You'd best get home now, before someone starts to worry about you." Sean noted that Cain had said "someone" as if he knew who that someone was as well as she did.

Caroline shot Cain a defiant look, then glanced again at Sean and smiled before turning and sauntering off along the path.

Sean started away as well, eager to free himself at once from an uncomfortable situation. "Good night, Sheriff," he nodded politely.

"Surprisin' you'd be casting your net so soon, Preacher," Cain commented before Sean could move out of earshot.

Sean stopped and turned back to the Sheriff. "I do not appreciate what you're implying, sir."

Cain moved a little closer, though Sean noted he was still careful to keep his distance.

"Then you won't like what I have to say next, either," he warned, "I heard you're invitin' folks to that meetin' house. You should know that Judge Wycherley paid to have some repairs made to it when the last preacher came through. Until that debt's been paid, he owns the place."

Sean didn't blink, though he felt a hint of anger rising up inside his chest. "A meeting house belongs to the people who fill it, and to God."

Cain chuckled and shook his head. "Judge Franklin Wycherley is the only God with any pull around here, Preacher. If it's in the Fourth Township, he pretty well owns it. Don't expect to see too many worshippers at church until your Methodist chiefs back in New York have paid the debt."

Cain turned and began to walk away, then swung back around to face Sean. "By the way, you'd best stay away from Caroline Wycherley. You're playin' with fire with that one. Besides, from what I've seen you've got yourself quite an eyeful waitin' for you back in that little shanty. If you can't satisfy her on a night like this, somebody else just might."

Instinct took over and Sean moved menacingly toward Cain, but at the same moment, Willem stepped out of the darkness between them. His intense stare was enough to give Sean pause.

"Let it be, Preacher," he said calmly, "As much as I'd like to see you have a go at him, you're a man of God, and the people of this settlement need to know that."

Sean glared at Cain, then stepped back, dropping his hands to his sides.

Cain seemed to relax then, shrugging and tipping his hat to them. "Good night, gentlemen," he grinned, before turning and walking back up the hill toward the path.

Sean exhaled loudly and attempted to smooth out his jacket.

"Looks like you could use a drink, Preacher," Willem observed.

*****

The men relaxed at the table in the cozy Hollister cabin, and Eliza quickly prepared a pot of dandelion tea. The children were all fast asleep, a long day of fresh air and chores behind them.

Eliza poured the tea and went about tidying up at the sink.

"This somehow isn't the kind of drink I was expecting you to offer, Willem," Sean smiled.

Willem grinned. "Eliza won't allow anything stronger in the house anymore."

Sean glanced over and caught Eliza's smile. He paused and took a sip of tea.

"Are you two always up this late?" he wondered.

"Only when there's people about to keep us awake," Willem hinted with a wink.

Sean set down his cup and looked again in Eliza's direction, "I do apologize for the fuss, Mrs. Hollister."

"It's quite alright, Reverend Brody," she nodded, setting down a cleaning cloth and turning back to the table, "Though I do think it's time I retire. Good night, gentlemen."

She patted Willem on the shoulder and quickly disappeared through a small door at the back of the cabin.

When she had gone, Willem spoke first.

"Your hands bear the marks of a hard life, Preacher," he

remarked, glancing at Sean's scarred fingers as he set down his tea.

"I was once a stage boxer," Sean confessed, nodding, "Miraculously my hands bore the brunt of the fights and my face still reveals a handsome man."

"That's a matter of opinion, isn't it?" Willem chided, and they both laughed. "Whatever made you go from that to being a man of God?" he asked.

Sean shifted uncomfortably in his chair. "I came close to death only once," he admitted, "And you might say I had a revelation."

"You saw God?" Willem wondered.

Sean shook his head. "I saw the end of my own life," he explained, "And I realized I wasn't ready for it. When I recovered, I felt a new sense of purpose."

"Every man needs such an awakening," Willem nodded.

"Amen," Sean agreed.

"Sheriff Cain is a dangerous man, Sean," Willem said quietly, "He's Franklin Wycherley's henchman. You did well to stop me last evening."

"The same can be said of you tonight," Sean replied, "But why is there any need for a henchman – much less a Sheriff at all in the Fourth Township?"

Willem sighed. "Wycherley came up here just after the Hungry Year ended around 1789, but he wasn't like the rest of us. We were all Loyalists and soldiers. He was a Whig, through and through, and we all knew it. He played along 'cause the British wanted more settlers, and they were offering free land to anyone who would take the oath of allegiance. So he did that, 'cause to him, it wasn't about loyalty, it was about land. He only had two hundred acres to start, but he brought slaves with him."

"They applied for land, too?" Sean guessed.

Willem nodded. "Those poor folks barely had time to start clearing brush before they started disappearing. Those who didn't vanish eventually ran off. Wycherley took over their land, and now he owns more property than any decent man in Adolphustown could have the strength to clear in a lifetime."

Sean shook his head, "He doesn't own you, Willem. He doesn't own your family or the ground you live on."

Willem was quiet for a moment, gathering his thoughts.

"We've had hard times here, Sean," he said. "The British didn't figure the war would last so long or cost so much. The last thing a man wants is to be dependent on someone else, but you change your mind fast when your wife and child are starving, when winter sets in and you're still living in a tent. At one time or another, most of us have promised to give Wycherley a measure of our crops or businesses in return for his help, and they become his until we can make good on it. I'm afraid he does own pieces of this place and the people in it, Sean, whether we like it or not."

CHAPTER FIVE

Charlotte stood near Sean, watching him prepare his horses for the trip to Kingston.

"Must you leave again so soon?" she pleaded, holding his hat in her hands, "There is still so much to be done here."

Sean finished fastening the saddlebags to his lead horse, then turned to his wife. "And you can do much of it, Mrs. Brody," he winked. "I agree that there is much for me to do as Superintendent of the Bay of Quinte circuit, and this journey is part of it."

Charlotte looked away.

"When I return," he continued, "I shall conduct my first sermon, and we need a willing hearer on every bench. So while I am gone, it will be up to you to encourage every resident of Adolphustown to take the Methodist road." He paused before adding, "I depend on you for this, Mrs. Brody."

Charlotte attempted her best optimistic smile, "Of course, Sean."

She handed him his hat and he leaned down to kiss her, hesitating when she quickly turned her head so that his lips would only meet her cheek. He paused, nodded, then straightened up. "And where is my Little Abigail?" he wondered.

"Here, Papa!" Abigail skipped into view from where she'd been playing with Emma nearby. "How long will you be gone, Papa?"

"A few days," Sean told her, squatting down to her level. "You must be a good girl and help your mother while I am away."

"I will!" she exclaimed.

Sean touched a finger to her nose, then followed it with a kiss.

He stood up and turned to climb up into the saddle, but Charlotte reached out for his hand. "Take this, Mr. Brody," and she offered him a few of her father's coins.

"There will be no reason for--" Sean began.

"You will be in Kingston!" she insisted, tucking a small note into his pocket, "Here is a list. You may see something we need, Sean. I have imposed on Eliza long enough. And furthermore, I expect to see you pulling the wagon behind you when you return. That, or I will walk to it myself and cart things back."

Sean reluctantly deposited the coins into his pocket and mounted up.

"Until I see you next, then," he nodded, placing his hat on his head.

"Until then," she confirmed dutifully.

"Good bye, Papa!" Abigail beamed, and he tipped his hat to her before riding away on the path that led west away from their shanty and out toward the Front. From there, he would follow the main road along the water straight into Kingston. Thanks to being more heavily travelled, it was easier to navigate than the crude forest path that had been blazed east from the Hollister's cabin. The tiny pathway was used as a shortcut mainly by natives and hardy souls willing to brave the thick brush and mosquitoes.

"Is he leaving you?" Charlotte heard a small voice ask, and she turned to see Emma standing there beside Abigail.

"Mr. Brody has important work, Emma," she said, crouching down to brush the child's long brown hair back from her face, but as she stood up and turned to watch Sean disappear along the path, she couldn't help but secretly despair that perhaps her husband's work was going to need to be more important than his family for some time

*****

Sean was making solid progress along the road, riding one horse while leading the other behind. His weight was too great for one animal to bear for long, especially along the almost impassable trails he sometimes encountered, and so he'd devised this method of travel whenever two horses were available. His journeys were as much a trial for them as it was for him, travelling through swamps and crossing rivers where there were no bridges, though he never complained. He was grateful to be able to deliver God's message to those who might not otherwise hear it.

He'd passed the wagon a few miles back. It was still undisturbed, from what he'd seen, though the mud was now dried around the wheels. It would take some work to pull it out. He'd slid down from his saddle to post a note to the side of the wagon inviting all to worship beginning the first Sunday in June, and he intended to be back in good time at the beginning of the week in order to be sure his first all-important sermon was ready. He slapped at another mosquito and wiped his sweaty brow, deciding to sing a hymn to keep his spirits up.

"O for a thousand tongues to sing my great redeemer's praise! The glories of my God and King, the triumphs of his grace! My gracious Master, and my God, assist me to proclaim, to spread through all the earth abroad the honours of thy name--"

Sean spotted an obese man dressed completely in black, puffing along toward him on foot. The man's face was as round as a tomato and just as red, though Sean didn't know if that was from exposure to the spring sun, or the sheer exertion of his travels. One thing was certain, he was not in a singing mood, and he muttered away unhappily under his breath as he trudged along.

He must have seen Sean coming his way, but chose not to look up, occupying himself instead with taking out a pocket watch and opening it to check the time.

Sean slowed his horse to a stop, tipping his preacher's hat to the stranger. "Good day, sir! May I be of some assistance? Perhaps the loan of a horse might be to your advantage?"

The man was forced to look up. "I hardly think a small elephant could carry my weight," he grumbled, "Let alone a mere pony such as the one you ride. Besides, you're going in the opposite direction to me."

"Adolphustown is not far back," Sean offered.

"Immediate transportation to the next village by buggy would be the only assistance I should accept," the man interrupted, shaking his head, "Though even the Anglican Bishop himself cannot take the time to supply me with a proper buggy, and even if he would, it would never survive these detestable roads, so what would be the point in asking?"

"You are an Anglican missionary, sir?" Sean asked with interest.

The man finally stopped walking, turning back. "Josiah Hamm," he offered, rather suspiciously. "And you?"

"I am the Reverend Sean Brody, newly-appointed Superintendent of the Bay of Quinte circuit."

Hamm's eyes widened. "A saddlebagger! I should have known." He shook his head again and continued on his way.

"Sir!" Sean called out, pulling on the reins to turn his horse in

Hamm's direction, "I wonder if we might endeavor to join hands in friendship?"

Hamm turned back and pointed a finger at Sean. "You and your Methodist teachings are encouraging division in the Lord's flock! I cannot converse with you any longer, much less accept any friendship with you. Please, keep at your own side of the road, sir, and be on your way!"

Sean sat for a few moments, watching Hamm waddle along the path until he was out of sight. Small wonder that the people of Adolphustown were losing faith, he thought to himself, if the likes of Hamm were all they had to cling to.

*****

Charlotte leaned down and picked up a bible that had been lying hidden beneath a bench. She ran her hand along the cover and glanced around the church. The dusting alone had taken so much longer than she'd expected it would. She'd been at it for the better part of the morning, and still she felt it might never be clean. Yet she knew she had to manage it somehow. There would be no help from Sean, now that he was on his way to Kingston to meet with Ezra Beckett. So it would be left to her to ensure the meeting house was at least presentable to those few who might attend services. Perhaps if they saw that their place of worship was open to them again, the settlers would be more inclined to welcome the Lord back into their lives, in spite of Judge Wycherley's threats and intimidation.

She set the bible on the bench, then sat down and stared ahead at the small wooden cross that was affixed to the front of the lectern. Her eyes filled with sadness as she thought again of what they'd left behind. New York was still a far enough jaunt from Vermont, but at least the odd trip home had been possible. Here, there was no hope of visits. She trusted that Sean would continue to find a way to take care of her and Abigail, and yet she missed the comfort of knowing that her parents were close enough to come to her aid if she needed them. She missed Daniel and Janey…beautiful Janey. Surely she would never find a friend such as her in Adolphustown.

"A good dip in the bay is what this place needs!"

Charlotte jumped when she heard the friendly voice, wiping her eyes with her sleeve.

She turned and saw Eliza, flanked by her brood of children, each one holding a bucket, rag or broom. Abigail pushed to the front of the pack, grinning. "Hello, mama! We came to help!"

They worked for most of the day, and by the time they were done, Charlotte felt a renewed sense of hope for the church. She gazed out one of the freshly-cleaned windows toward the bay, and it seemed she had been given a new perspective on the world. She could see everything from the church more clearly now. The late afternoon sun hung lazily over the smooth waters of the bay. Perhaps this task that she originally thought would be so daunting had cleansed not just the church, but her soul as well.

She insisted that Eliza and the children stay out of the Hollister kitchen and let her prepare their supper when they finally arrived home, exhausted. They were all gathered around the table, just settling down to eat, when Willem walked in and glanced at the group. They all stayed quiet, and Charlotte sensed it was because they feared he knew they had helped her at the meeting house.

The family waited in silence while Willem finished at the washbasin, then proceeded to pull out his chair and sit in his spot at the head of the table. "You make sure those buckets and rags got put back?" he asked Eliza, and Charlotte held her breath.

"Yes, Willem," Eliza smiled obediently, "And the children rinsed everything when we were done."

"The church looks beautiful clean, Papa," Emma piped up, "Thank you for allowing us to help Mrs. Brody."

Charlotte saw Willem's face suddenly soften. He looked down at his plate, thinking, then nodded. "Maybe tomorrow morning you can take me and show me what you did, Emma," he said slowly, "I'd like to see it."

"Tomorrow's Thursday, Papa," Phoebe reminded him in a responsible tone, "You'll be needed at the tavern."

Willem picked up his fork. "The tavern will still be there by afternoon, Phoebe," he nodded, "I expect it can wait."

Emma and Abigail grinned happily, and Charlotte exchanged a surprised glance with Eliza. Perhaps there was more than an ounce of hope left in this desperate settlement after all.

****

The Kingston market was bustling with activity. Vendors chatted with shoppers as children dashed in and out of stalls. Sean took it all in, stopping outside a stone house just on the edge of the market. There he dismounted and tied his horses to a hitching post.

A boy stood nearby, gazing up at the huge man before him.

"Will you watch them for me?" Sean asked, squatting down to be closer to the boy, and he reached into his pocket and produced a coin as payment.

The boy smiled and nodded his head. "I'll watch them, yes sir!"

Sean tossed him the coin and stood up, making his way toward the main door to the market house. He passed a small wooden sign that read, "Kingston Methodist Chapel", and almost immediately heard a booming voice, "Come, ye weary sinners, come, come, ye guilty spirits oppressed, answer to the Saviour's call, come, and I will give you rest, come, and I will save you all!"

Sean uncomfortably brushed past a harlot and her admirer as they pressed against one another. Nearby, a shabbily-clothed vagabond begged for whatever passers-by might spare him. Pushing through a small crowd of people, he glanced over and finally saw Ezra Beckett standing upon a butcher's block. He knew it was Beckett based on a description he'd been given by Bishop Weston before leaving New York. A young man with fair hair that hung loosely to his shoulders, Beckett was passionate in his cause and had been blessed with a fair countenance that, had he not been pious, might easily have led him into much temptation. Instead, he had stayed the course, and now used his gift for oration to bring not just adoring young women, but also many curious men who had gathered around the butcher's block.

"Jesus, full of truth and love," Beckett continued, "We thy kindest word obey; faithful let thy mercies prove, take our load of guilt away!"

Still, not everyone in the crowd was happy with the preacher's teachings.

"Away with you!" came a shout; "We don't want your Methodist blasphemy here!" yelled another.

Undeterred, Ezra continued on, eventually glancing down and

noticing Sean. A look of faint familiarity crossed his face, and when Sean reached up, removed his hat and flipped it over in his hand, Ezra smiled, jumping down from the block. "Brother, I would gather that you are the Reverend Sean Brody!" he exclaimed, approaching.

"The Bishop told me you would quickly spot me if I made a sign with my hat." Sean flipped it over in his hand again and then placed it back on his head. "This sign has made me familiar to others upon first meeting as well," he continued.

Ezra smiled. "Ah, 'twas not the hat, but the man beneath it that I recognized!"

He reached up and patted Sean on the back before pointing off in the direction of the chapel. "I have received only one letter from the American Conference regarding your impending arrival," Beckett explained as they walked, "In it, I was advised to look for a very large man. The hat was not a necessary indicator."

Sean smiled. "The only description provided me of you was of a man," and he cleared his throat rather dramatically before continuing, "possessed of a voice so sweet that he can serenade even the most desperate of heathens into a life of repentance."

Beckett chuckled. "Well, perhaps between your extraordinary muscular developments and my songbird-like exhortations, we can finally begin to find some converts among these, shall we say, uncivilized masses."

Sean nodded as he followed Ezra inside the chapel. "That is my sincere hope as well, brother Beckett."

*****

By Friday morning, Charlotte felt she'd had enough of obligatory visits with townsfolk who slammed their doors and drew their curtains when they saw her approach the doorstep. However she knew that Sean would need a full report upon his return, and even if the news was not what he might want to hear, she was determined to let him know that she had done her part as the preacher's wife.

"Mrs. Braswell?" she inquired as the door slowly creaked open.

"Who's askin'?" came the suspicious reply.

Charlotte could only see the woman's dark eyes peering furtively around the half-open door, and she braced herself for an onslaught of cuss words, then took a small step back, just in case the door flew shut without warning. "I am the Reverend Sean Brody's wife," she announced.

The woman hesitated, then finally pulled the door open the rest of the way, and Charlotte's senses came alive with the smell of the strange cooking odor wafting out of the house.

"Come in!" the woman urged, "We can't have everything escaping out the door!"

Charlotte stepped in quickly, jumping a bit when Mrs. Braswell slammed the door hard behind her. Glancing around, she was reminded of the Apothecary not far along the street from her parents' home. Jars and vials covered the table, some filled with dark-coloured liquids, others half full of various plants and weeds. Dried herbs hung everywhere from the ceiling. The smell wasn't unpleasant, but far from flowery. She saw a pot simmering over the fire, and moved a little closer, trying to see what was cooking.

"It's only dandelion tea," Mrs. Braswell laughed, waving Charlotte toward a chair near the window, "What did you think?"

Charlotte felt her face flush with embarrassment as she sat down, "Forgive me, Mrs. Braswell," she smiled, "It does not smell like dandelion tea."

"Oh, well that's all the things I've just finished cooking and put in the jars," the woman explained, "You're lucky my Calvin's not home yet with the fish. They really stink up the place."

Picking up a metal ladle and cup from the table, she moved to the pot and scooped out some tea. She paused, then smiled, "It's Betsey, by the way."

Charlotte nodded when she was handed the cup. "Thank you. I'm Charlotte."

She saw a jar full of dandelion stems on the small table beside her. "You use it in something other than tea," she observed.

"Not sure why I bother with it," Betsey replied, shrugging, "As long as you keep with the dandelion tea, your innards should stay healthy." She looked closer at Charlotte, "In fact," she continued, "I have something for you."

She stood up and went to a tall cabinet, opened the door in the top, and sorted through one, then another of the jars until she found what she was looking for. She turned back to Charlotte, who set her tea cup carefully on the table near the dandelions before accepting the small jar in her hand.

"Stinging nettles," Betsey explained before Charlotte had a chance to ask, "Good for your weariness," she finished.

Charlotte set the small jar on the table near the dandelions, then gazed back up at Betsey "How could you have known that I--"

"Anyone can see you're worn through, Mrs. Brody,' she answered, "And that concoction will help with your monthly complaints, too. It'll clean things out to make way for babies."

Charlotte shuffled uncomfortably in her chair. "We already have a child," she nodded.

"And there will be more," Betsey smiled, "But first you need to give your body and your mind some rest. Take a swallow of that mixture once each morning and night."

Charlotte did not think that Sean would approve, but she wouldn't let Mrs. Braswell know. "Thank you," she said, "My nanny often prepared similar remedies when I was a child. Cealy was always out picking different kinds of berries when they came ripe."

"Elderberries are still quite a ways off," Betsey commented absently, glancing out the window, "You can't eat them when you pick them, though. You have to boil them first."

"What are they used for?" Charlotte asked, interested.

"For elderberry wine!" Betsey answered, and this time they both chuckled.

Charlotte placed her gloved hands on the arms of the chair and set her mind to business. "Mrs. Braswell - Betsey, I do not know if you and your husband have frequented the Methodist meeting house in the past--"

"We haven't," Betsey cut her off, "And we don't intend to."

"But why?" Charlotte wondered, almost pleading.

"Why should we?" the woman asked, incredulous, "Most folks around here think I'm evil." She shook her head, "No, Calvin and I don't have much to do with neighbours or religion, and nobody in all the land, even if they're sweet as you are, will ever convince us to."

CHAPTER SIX

It was late afternoon, but the day was still hot as Sean directed his horse away from the Front and onto the side road that would take him to the back of the settlement, and home. Thirsty from the heat, he stopped and dismounted not far from where he and Charlotte had abandoned the wagon, pulling a canteen from the saddlebag. He'd had a good visit with Brother Beckett. Their regular morning market exhortations had resulted in several new converts. Two backsliders who had fallen away from the church had also been reclaimed. Sean hoped this was indicative of things to come in Adolphustown as well. He knew there were a number of backsliders in the Fourth Township, due in no small part to Judge Wycherley's evil influence, but the settlement had been without a Methodist leader for long enough. His time with Ezra had refueled Sean's ambitions, and he had already decided that once he had resumed regular services at the church, he would also begin to make plans for the Bay of Quinte's first-ever camp meeting in the fall.

Sean glanced ahead to where his wagon still sat, just off to the side of the path. This would be a good opportunity to finally dig it out. He knew that Charlotte would be happier to see him if she saw their remaining possessions were with him as well. He led the horses over near the wagon and tied them to a tree in the shade, then began to inspect how far down the wheels were embedded. As he leaned over, a branch snapped in the woods, and unfamiliar bird calls suddenly rose up around him.

Sean straightened up and glanced into the nearby woods. He knew from many years as an itinerant preacher that what he was hearing were not normal forest sounds. There were natives nearby, and they had already spotted him.

He sensed someone behind him and instinctively swung around just as a tall Mohawk man stepped onto the road. The Bishop had warned him that the Iroquois of this area were a fierce-looking tribe, but Sean found it difficult to fear the handsome young man who stood before him, his dark complexion free of any paint or decoration. His long dark hair was tied neatly back behind his neck, somehow making his high cheekbones and strong jaw even more pronounced. A crisp white shirt was tied at his waist with a belt, and his leggings were not made of leather, but cloth. Perhaps, Sean thought to himself, this was due to the influence of the constant tide of white settlers moving into the Bay of Quinte area.

Colourful feathers danced on the man's moccasin boots as he took a couple of steps forward and motioned toward the canteen. Sean swiftly handed it over and watched the Mohawk empty it, then drop it gently onto the ground before motioning toward the woods.

Sean hesitated, more out of confusion than panic. "I...I don't understand. Do you speak English?"

"I would like to show you something in the forest," the man announced, and Sean was surprised to hear him speak English so smoothly.

"I am afraid I must refuse," Sean protested, taking a step back toward his horses, "My wife is waiting for me."

"You have a wife," the young man nodded, "Maybe she needs this."

Sean paused, waiting to see him produce a trinket or native jewellery out of his pocket, but instead, he turned and shouted to someone in the forest. "Albert! Albert!"

Albert was young, probably only a teenager. When he stepped out onto the path, Sean could not help but begin to chuckle, and it was not due to the fact that the young man's scalp was plucked to a smooth, shiny finish with the exception of one long, stiff line of hair running along the middle of his head. This scalp lock style actually looked quite fierce on men with serious faces, but Albert simply appeared unhappy. His mouth was downturned in a miserable frown, and Sean surmised the reason was probably due to the fact that the youngster was wearing a long, decorative native frock.

"It will look better on your wife," the taller one suggested.

"I should have to agree with you there," Sean nodded, trying to hold back his grin.

"I will not beg for your money," the tall man promised, "But if you buy the frock, you will help my village."

Sean still had the coins Charlotte had given him in his pocket, and he knew it was more money than he would have occasion to spend between here and Adolphustown.

"Very well then," he finally conceded, "If this will mean that I can be on my way..."

He turned and walked to the lead horse, reaching into his saddlebag and pulling out a few coins, which he turned and offered to the men. "What is your price, sir?"

The tall one moved closer and glanced at the coins, a look of alarm spreading across his face. Sean recognized the danger signal immediately and took a step backward, but now Albert also moved forward to see the coins in Sean's outstretched hand.

"Yankee! Yankee!" he shouted, jumping up and down excitedly. He turned to his friend, "Degan! A yankee!"

Sean tried to calm him down. "Please, gentlemen. There is no need for excitement."

At first he did not feel alarmed. In fact, it was somewhat absurd to see the beads on Albert's dress shaking wildly out of control as he ran to hide behind Degan, who kept his eyes on Sean as he bent down to slip a knife from his boot.

Albert turned and fled back into the forest, and Sean prayed he wasn't running to find others who could help.

Degan waved the knife through the air in front of Sean's face. He may have been nearly a foot shorter, but he was a mighty foe with that sharp weapon in his skilled hand as he moved in a circle around Sean.

"Yankees are an enemy to my people," he warned.

"The war is long over, sir," Sean reminded him, "It's Degan, isn't it? I assure you, Degan, that I am a peaceful man of God."

When he mentioned the Lord's name, Sean thought he saw a glint of understanding flicker in the Mohawk's eye, but just as suddenly, it disappeared.

"You are nothing but a Yankee!" Degan shouted, and thrust the knife toward Sean, cutting his hand and drawing blood as the coins fell to the ground. Sean glanced at him, surprised that it had come to this. Degan thrust the knife again, but this time Sean skillfully reached out and flipped him down onto the ground, forcing the weapon out of his hand.

Degan struggled, but Sean held tight, moving his hands up toward the man's neck and beginning to squeeze. He stared into Degan's pleading eyes, but a foreboding darkness began to seep into his soul, and he found he could not stop clutching at the helpless man's neck. He was angry. Angry at Charlotte for not trusting him through everything. Angry at the Bishop for sending him to such a place as this when it was England that should have called to him. He heard his father's dreaded voice, felt the sting of the branches again, felt Degan slapping at his chest to get his attention. Sean's hands were clamped around his neck. A hundred prize fights flashed in his mind. He knew how easy it would be to kill this man, and in a wilderness like this, there might never be a price to pay. Men took other men's lives every day and were never held accountable.

He heard Degan struggling to catch his breath, and luckily it was enough to lead Sean to loosen his grip. When he let go, he jumped up, breathing heavy, and backed away. Degan's neck and collar were streaked with blood, and Sean was relieved to realize it was only from his own injured hand.

He leaned over and grabbed the knife from the ground as his foe, coughing and gasping, slowly managed to stand up.

"Why didn't you kill me, Yankee?" Degan sputtered weakly.

Catching his breath, Sean shook his head. "I have no wish to kill you, my friend. I am the Reverend Sean Brody of Adolphustown. I have no quarrel with you, nor with any Upper Canadian. I would like to be your friend."

The man's eyes went wide with suspicion, and he reached up to touch his neck, where Sean could now see the faint outline of his handprints. "Mr. Hamm is our preacher," Degan informed him.

"Then he is a fortunate man to have such a devoted follower," Sean nodded. "Keep the coins. I have no use for them. It is obvious to me now more than ever that they are indeed the devil's temptation."

Sean tossed the knife on the ground at Degan's feet, then untied the horses and began to lead them away.

"That is my wagon," he said, pointing toward it as he walked, "I am far too tired to dig it out now, but if you and your friend can somehow manage to bring it to Adolphustown, I have more coins there that I can give you." Sean held his breath, hoping the men would allow him to leave without any further trouble.

"I am Degan Hawke," the man called after him, "You will see me again."

*****

The day had seemed like an eternity to Charlotte, finishing the washing, cleaning the Hollister boys' fish catch, and baking bread in the heat of the kitchen. She was grateful when Eliza offered to have Abigail for supper, and not being hungry herself, she slipped inside the shanty and plopped down onto the bed, exhausted. At almost the same moment, Sean stepped through the door. Charlotte did not have the energy to rise from the mattress to see to him, though she did raise her head just enough to see that he was carrying books, which he set on the table.

"We will see this through, Charlotte," he told her, "God will see us through it."

"We should have never left New York," she replied groggily, managing to sit up.

"I had no choice, Charlotte--"

"You left us with no choice!" she raised her voice, and regaining her vigor, she stood up to face him. "Bishop Weston banished you here because you could not keep your fists to yourself! You willingly inflicted pain and injury upon others in the name of greed! You, of all people Sean, gave in to the Devil's temptation. And then you proceeded to use your winnings to purchase a sounding board and hymnals!"

She moved to the table and picked up a book, took a moment to make sure it was not his bible, and then swiftly hurled it in his direction. He barely stepped out of the way as she continued, unflinching. "You blackened your own name and that of your church. And now here we are without friends, without family, without hope!" She stood there, her blazing eyes fixed on him, waiting for him to make some excuse.

Sean merely stared back at her, stunned, before finally asking the obvious, "You knew?"

"Did you think I would not wonder how we suddenly were able to have the things we needed, the things we wanted?"

"Yet you did not put a stop to it," he said quietly.

Charlotte's head dropped a little. She looked away from him. "It's true," she admitted, "My silence implicated me in the wrongdoing as well, and I am smaller because of it, Mr. Brody."

She looked up at him and saw that his eyes were filled with regret. "Did you find a dress for Abigail?" she asked, trying to change the subject.

"There was little time for shopping, Charlotte--"

"Then give me the coins and I shall stop into Hanley's General Store tomorrow. They have just had delivery of some new fabric. I am sure Eliza will lend me some sewing supplies. And perhaps there will be some real tea--"

"The coins you gave me are gone," Sean admitted.

"What?" Charlotte shouted, shocked. "How?"

"It does not matter now, Charlotte," Sean shook his head, "The Lord will provide for us--"

"Tell that to our daughter while she eats soup I've made from tree bark, Mr. Brody!"

Frustrated, Charlotte threw her arms up in the air, but as she moved toward the door, Sean reached out and gently pulled her back, leading her to the table. He sat down and pulled another chair over beside him, motioning for her to join him. Charlotte plopped down reluctantly beside him, but she would not look at him.

"I know this has all been very difficult for you, darling," he told her, reaching for her hand. He paused, then asked, smirking, "You have not really been forced to make soup from tree bark, have you?"

Charlotte pulled away from him. "I want to go back to Vermont immediately," she insisted, unamused.

He thought for a moment before saying, "I will tell you what, Mrs. Brody. I will go into the woods and pray for guidance."

"Now?" Charlotte exclaimed "You have only just arrived home, Sean."

"This is the only way," he answered, and he stood, picked up his bible from the table, and left the shanty.

Evening wore on, and even long after Abigail returned home from her meal at the Hollister's, there was still no sign of Sean.

"Where is Papa? Abigail wondered.

"I am sure he will be along soon," Charlotte soothed, leaning down to tuck Abigail's long hair behind her ears, "For now, you must sleep, and perhaps your father will be here when you awake."

Abigail smiled and stretched up on her tiptoes to kiss her mother's cheek, then turned and happily ran to her mattress. "The faster I fall asleep, the more quickly Papa will arrive!" she grinned, crawling under her covers and pulling them up to her neck.

Charlotte did not have the energy to direct her daughter to change into her night clothes. Instead, she went to the window and stared out into the night, hoping that Sean would soon return. The wild forest was certainly no place for anyone in the darkness. She regretted their argument. She regretted admitting that she was ready to give up and go home to Vermont. Sean needed her to be strong, and she was failing him.

The next morning he walked through the door as if nothing out of the ordinary had happened, as if men go into the forest and pray among the beasts every night.

Charlotte, having hardly slept, gratefully rose from their bed and went to him. Abigail did the same, and Sean took them into his arms. Kissing them both, he paused and looked into Charlotte's eyes. "I have just spent the entire night engaged in prayer, and I believe that God will send us help. If help does not come today, I will take you back to Vermont and I will go into any business that your father wishes."

Charlotte felt tears of relief welling up in her eyes, and she wrapped her arms around him again. "Thank you," she whispered.

After breakfast there was a knock upon the door, and Abigail ran to see who might be visiting.

"Does the preacher live here?" asked a voice familiar to Sean.

Abigail retreated back into the shanty, frightened, and grabbed onto her mother's skirts.

"What is it, little Abigail?" Charlotte wondered, glancing apprehensively toward the open door.

"Mr. Hawke!" Sean moved forward to extend a hearty welcome. "This is my wife, Charlotte, and my daughter Abigail," he smiled.

Degan nodded toward them and took a step forward, but Abigail slipped around behind her mother to hide completely.

"It's alright, little Abigail," Sean reassured her, "Degan is my friend."

Degan looked at Sean and nodded, then reached into the haversack that was slung over his shoulder and produced the beautiful native dress that Albert had been wearing in the forest. He held it out toward Charlotte, but before she could reach for it,

Abigail ran forward and grabbed it from him, quickly returning to safety at her mother's side.

Degan chuckled, then turned back to Sean. "We brought your wagon."

Sean's eyes widened and he followed Degan back outside, with Charlotte and Abigail not far behind. Albert stood proudly beside the wagon, its wheels still covered in hardened mud. He was holding the reins of the large horse that had pulled it to Adolphustown.

"You look as if you are feeling more like yourself today, Albert," Sean smiled, taking note of the young man's grey trousers and white fabric shirt. Albert turned his head to one side, not quite understanding, but Degan translated. Albert's eyes lit up with realization and he smiled, nodding at Sean in agreement.

"Thank you!" Charlotte spoke up, still holding her new dress as she moved forward, "We are ever so grateful!"

"Wait here," Sean told them, "And I will get those coins I promised--"

"No," Degan stopped him, "You are a preacher. The only payment you can give us is the word of God." He held up one of Sean's notes promoting the Sunday church service. "There may be some who would be interested to hear what you have to say, if you will come across the bay and tell us more."

Charlotte reached for Sean's hand and squeezed it as a handful of settlers gathered nearby, watching with interest.

"I am humbled by your friendship, sir," Sean nodded, "I will visit your home and speak to your community as you have requested."

Degan bowed his head slightly in reply, and as he turned to go, Caroline Wycherley appeared on the main path that led from the church. Sean saw her stop dead when she spotted the Mohawks, and he stepped forward, concerned that Cain might not be far behind her looking for trouble. "These men have brought our wagon," he proclaimed loudly to anyone who might hear, "And we are thankful to them. Go in peace, gentlemen," he encouraged.

Degan nodded, glanced at Caroline, and ushered Albert away toward the forest path.

Once they had disappeared into the trees, Sean threw back the tarp as he and Charlotte inspected the remaining contents of the wagon. "It all seems to be here," he nodded. He glanced at Charlotte and noticed that she seemed deep in thought. "What is it?" he wondered.

"I did not think that I would be the one to admit it, or that I would be the one to believe that it could happen," she replied, "But it does seem to appear that we have received a sign, Mr. Brody. Our sign from God."

*****

Charlotte began hanging the wash, the thought crossing her mind that the drying time would be swift, what with the strong wind that was blowing in off the bay. She glanced up at the clothesline, squinting in the sunlight as she hung another of Sean's shirts. She had barely been awake when he had risen and hurried out the door quite early, though she'd felt his soft kiss upon her forehead before he left. She supposed that he had made haste for the church, and she found it did not bother her quite as much as before to think that he would leave their bed and hurry off to attend to his duties. She felt a smile spread across her face, thinking back to the previous night. For the first time since they'd arrived in Adolphustown, she had allowed Sean to be her husband again in every way, and it felt like a fresh start.

"Mama! Mama!" Abigail approached excitedly and nearly out of breath, "Look what Papa is doing!"

Charlotte glanced up to the sky above the bay where Abigail was pointing, and her stomach fluttered with excitement at what she saw. Hurrying down to the shore, she joined several Adolphustown residents who stood staring out at the water in bewilderment. Charlotte clasped her hands to her chest, a smile spreading across her face.

Sean was being pulled gently through the water as he held tight to a long piece of twine leading up to a diamond-shaped kite, its long cotton tail blowing happily in the wind. Willem was walking along the shore, watching.

"They've been working on that thing outside the cabin for hours," Eliza commented, stepping near, "Peeling cedar off the trees and taking any bits of my linen and silk they could steal away with unseen." She grinned and turned to Charlotte, "They looked as proud as school boys when they were done."

Charlotte beamed and looked out again at Sean. "Mr. Brody!" she called out, laughing, and he turned his head slightly, taking his eyes away from the kite. He grinned when he saw her and Charlotte waved, her heart swelling with happiness.

CHAPTER SEVEN

Charlotte felt hopeful as she sat in the front bench, her hand wrapped around Abigail's. Sean paced back and forth in front of them, clutching a bible. The floor boards squeaked beneath his weight. Ignoring any potential threat from Franklin Wycherley, they'd arrived early to ready the church for his first service since their arrival in Adolphustown, and the first to be held at the meeting house in many months.

Sean stopped pacing and glanced at Charlotte. "You made it very clear that I would preach today?" he asked.

"Of course, Sean," she answered firmly, "Very clear."

He began to pace again. "Perhaps I should have waited another week," he muttered, half to himself, "I could have gone to the native settlement today instead. Something tells me there may be more willing hearers there."

"People will come, Sean," Charlotte encouraged.

"You had a sign, Papa," Abigail spoke up, "Remember?"

Sean stopped in front of them and grinned at his daughter, then leaned over to face her. "Yes, Little Abigail, you are right. There was definitely a sign." He reached out and placed his hand over theirs, and Charlotte's heart flooded with happiness. Her family was her life. Sean and Abigail were all she needed in this world. Her faith in them and in God would see her through this challenging time. Even this would pass.

Footsteps could be heard entering through the open doors and Sean rose to his feet. Charlotte swung around expectantly, hoping to see the doorway filled with townsfolk, but her hopes were dashed when she saw only three young men step inside. She did not recognize them from the settlement, but she was happy to see them just the same. Perhaps there were more people behind them.

They all looked to be fresh out of their teenage years, and none were dressed for meeting house, wearing simple long-sleeved shirts with sleeves rolled up as if they'd just come from working in the fields. The one on the left, wearing worn breeches and a dark waistcoat over his threadbare shirt, was noticeably shorter than the other two. His bushy blonde locks jutted out from beneath a soft felt hat, pulled down so much that it almost completely concealed his eyes. Still, Charlotte could see well enough that his gaze was dark and determined.

The man on the right reached up and nervously removed his tattered straw hat, glancing around the church and bowing his head a little. His straight, dark hair was pulled back in a ribbon, and Charlotte thought he somehow looked the most respectable of the three.

The middle one, the tallest and most solid of all of them, hiked up his trousers and took a step forward as Sean moved toward them in greeting. "Yes, come in, gentlemen," he smiled, waving them inside – please do leave the door open so that the breeze may cool the church in time for the arrival of others."

The tall one stopped, glanced quickly over his shoulder, then turned back to Sean with a smug look on his face. "Others?" he asked, "You think other people are coming?"

Charlotte felt a pang of fear in her chest, and she reached an arm around Abigail, pulling her tightly to her side. She could instantly see that Sean felt apprehensive as well, setting his bible down on the bench beside them as he stepped into the aisle and approached the men.

"If you are here to listen to the word of God, you are welcome," he told them, "But if you are here to make trouble, I must insist that you leave immediately."

"Face forward, Abigail," Charlotte instructed quietly, "And close your ears."

"I do not know how to do that, Mama," Abigail said honestly.

"You know what I mean," her mother whispered, and Abigail obediently clasped her hands over her ears.

Charlotte heard the scuffle of feet on the wood plank floor as the men moved closer to Sean, and she glanced around at the large windows, checking to see if any of them were open wide enough for her to push Abigail outside to run for help. Surely Willem would come if he knew what was happening. She turned her head to watch what was transpiring.

"We've been sent to tell you there won't be anyone coming today, or any day," the tall one announced.

"I need not ask who sent you," Sean nodded, but I will ask you to give him a message for me."

"What's the message?"

Sean moved forward, reached down and grabbed the man by the back of his trousers, swinging him around. The man's height did not help him, and nor, to Charlotte's relief, did his friends, each of whom quickly high-tailed it out of the church the moment they saw quick work being made of the most brazen among them. With his free hand, Sean clamped onto the back of the young man's shirt and, with a good grip at each point, lifted him into the air and easily walked to the open door, tossing him outside onto the ground in a heap.

"Can I open my ears now, Mama?" Abigail wondered.

"Yes," Charlotte nodded, watching the door as Sean stepped back inside, apparently unscathed, "Yes, darling, you may open your ears."

"There will not be a service next Sunday," Sean announced, returning to the front of the church to retrieve his bible, "If it is only the Mohawks who desire to hear me, then only the Mohawks shall benefit from my work here."

"It is not that the people do not want to hear you, Sean," Charlotte protested, "Perhaps if we wait a little longer--"

"No one is coming, Charlotte!" he shouted, and Abigail placed her hands over her ears again.

Seeing this, Sean took a deep breath and lowered his voice to its normal volume. "Judge Wycherley has frightened the people and kept them away, but I will not give in to his oppression." He paused, thinking, then said, "I need some air." He grabbed his books from the small table nearby and headed for the door.

"Are they gone?" Charlotte asked anxiously, glancing toward the back of the church as he went.

"As far and as fast as their young farmer's legs will take them," Sean nodded, then added, "But I shall wait for you outside in any case." He walked quickly out of the church, slamming the door shut with a thunderous bang.

"I will be surprised if that door survives the summer," Charlotte sighed, glancing down at Abigail.

They made their way home along the well-worn path, and as they walked, Charlotte glanced over toward each of the cabins, offering a wave when she saw a neighbour in their yard. She wasn't one to curse, but she silently seethed at the thought of Judge Wycherley. How dare he frighten these good people away from attending services? By now she was coming to be better acquainted with the settlers, learning their names, and their stories. She thought of the forthright Mrs. Braswell. Her medicinal wisdom could help many people in Adolphustown, if only they would open their minds and hearts to her.

Supper was a quiet affair. Charlotte was grateful to finally have her cooking supplies to work with, and Eliza had helped her learn how to use the bake kettle quite efficiently. Abigail helped her clean up when the meal was finished, but Sean sat quietly at the table, glancing across the room and out the window.

"What is that?" he asked, quite suddenly.

Charlotte turned to him, puzzled.

Sean rose to his feet and pushed the chair out behind him, hurrying to the door. Charlotte and Abigail excitedly followed him outside.

"There!" Sean exclaimed, "What is that flickering I see?"

Charlotte caught a quick glimpse of a torch flame as it disappeared into the thick tree line down along the shore, moving away from the settlement.

"It must be someone going to visit a neighbour," she decided.

"I don't think there are any houses down that way," Sean shook his head.

"It is not for us to wonder over our neighbour's business," she softly reminded him.

"Go back inside, Little Abigail," he instructed their daughter, and she swiftly did as she was told.

When she was safely out of earshot, Sean turned to Charlotte and almost whispered, "Reverend Beckett spoke of a sorceress who lives nearby. Perhaps this is some dark ritual in the woods."

Charlotte crossed her arms in front of her and let out an exasperated sigh. She was hesitant to tell Sean of her visit with Betsey Braswell, and yet she felt a need to speak up for her.

"I do not believe in such nonsense," she replied, "And I am surprised that you do, Sean."

"One never knows," he countered, shaking his head and glancing back toward the now darkened shore, "It could be that there is far more work to be done here than first we thought."

*****

The following Sunday, Sean set out early for the Mohawk settlement on the other side of the bay. He had planned to leave a day early on horseback until Degan suggested that the journey would be considerably shortened by water. Charlotte and Abigail accompanied him to the church to watch him leave, and it was an incredible sight, witnessing the arrival of a small flotilla of Mohawk canoes. Degan pulled the lead canoe up onto shore and waited.

Sean turned to Charlotte. "I hope to be home by supper," he told her, "But do not wait for me if I tarry. You may open the church this morning if you please, and if anyone does appear, lead them in song and fellowship and explain that I will return to preach next Sunday."

"Yes, Sean," she nodded, lifting Abigail's hand and placing it in her father's.

He leaned down and kissed his daughter on the forehead. "Take good care of your mother," he instructed.

"I will feed her no cornbread," Abigail promised, then smiled and tapped her father's nose with her finger.

Sean laughed and straightened up, pulling Charlotte to him. "We are truly blessed, my darling," he whispered, and she wrapped her arms around him in response.

The natives paddled swiftly, so accustomed were they to canoe travel, and Sean quickly saw the benefits of making the trip by water. If the journey were necessary in winter, he could cross on the ice as he had many times during his itinerant travels throughout his circuit. He did not relish the thought of traversing frozen bays in winter, swamplands and bogs in the spring, and mosquito-infested forests in the heat of the summer, but if it was the only way to deliver God's word to those who were too far afield to attend meeting house to hear a sermon, he would continue to be a willing traveller.

Upon reaching the shores of the Mohawk settlement, Sean looked up the embankment and saw a few cabins here and there, quite similar to the structures in Adolphustown. Some were cruder than others, but it appeared that the day of the longhouse was over. He was pleased to see that the natives had already established such a thriving community.

"We have learned by watching the settlers in Adolphustown,"

Degan explained, pulling open his cabin door and motioning for Sean to step inside, "Yet we don't do everything as they do, because not everything they do makes sense."

"We can all learn from one another," Sean agreed, glancing around the large living space that was Degan's home. He thought how Charlotte would appreciate the massive fireplace with the smooth brick hearth surrounding it. Raised benches on either side of the cabin were covered in furs and blankets for sleeping comfort, and the morning sun beamed in through glass window panes.

"Your wife must be happy here," Sean commented.

Degan paused thoughtfully, then shook his head. "I built it to make a wife happy," he answered, "But as of yet, I have no one to share this place with."

Sean was puzzled. "But I see many women here."

"Women are a mystery, Reverend Brody," Degan marvelled, "Even Mohawk women."

Chickens squawked, scattering out of their way as they walked toward the main part of the settlement where the people had been asked to gather to hear Sean speak. Degan pointed over toward fields of freshly-sown maize, beans, and squash, planted in mounds of soil.

"They are good for each other," Degan said, "So we plant them together."

Small children giggled, following behind them as they walked.

"This is a peaceful place," Sean observed.

"Peace is important to us," Degan nodded. "My parents named me after a legendary Peacekeeper, Deganawida. He brought many Iroquois tribes together."

"It is a good name," Sean smiled.

In front of their cabins, men were cleaning fish with metal knives, the women busy scrubbing china dishes in wash buckets.

"We trade wild game and furs at the trading post near Adolphustown," Degan explained, "Sometimes we trade for flintlock rifles, sometimes for scissors and thimbles." He grinned, "Which means that the women can make many more dresses for Albert. Unfortunately for him."

Sean laughed and nodded in reply as they approached a clearing where those who were interested had gathered in a circle, many of them sitting on blankets. Some were standing, perhaps not quite yet convinced that they would stay for long. Degan went to the middle of the circle and made the introduction, inviting Sean to come to the centre to begin his sermon.

Sean knew that Josiah Hamm had already made Anglican inroads here, but there could still be those who were ready to hear God's word delivered in a new way. He held his bible high in the air and began a loud and passionate sermon. He understood that the proud Mohawks might be as difficult to convert as Charlotte's Baptist parents, but he would spread the word here just the same. These people needed to hear his message just as much as the people of Adolphustown did.

As he exhorted about finding the path to Heaven, Sean noticed a handful of women begin to break into sobs, crying out to the skies above in their native language, their arms reaching upward. When he was finished, he turned to Degan. "What are they saying?" he asked.

"They have been moved by your words," Degan replied, "And they wonder if they have been wrong to listen to Mr. Hamm. They are worried that they may not be allowed to go into Heaven now, and they are confused. They think their ancestors could not have gone to Heaven, because they went into the sunset many years before you or Mr. Hamm were even known to us."

Sean paused and took a deep breath, reminding himself that he had prepared for this. "No!" he called out over the sound of the wailing women, "No!" he yelled again, and this time he raised his voice so loudly that they were compelled to cease their crying, staring at him through their tears.

"God wants you to know that he loves you, every one of you!" Sean announced, addressing each of them directly and pointing to each of them as he did so. "God created the sunset, did he not?" The women exchanged glances. He watched them carefully, confident that he had their rapt attention.

"Yes," Sean encouraged, "Your ancestor's sunset is also my Heaven. If you follow God's word, I believe that you will see your families again in your sunset, in Heaven."

Slowly their eyes began to show understanding.

"You must tell us more," one of them requested, "We need to learn more, Preacher."

*****

After sharing a meal with the elders, Sean followed Degan down to the shore toward the canoes. As he walked, he reflected on the day and decided that there were many who had gratefully received his message, including his friend Degan.

"I feel something new in my heart," Degan had admitted, "I look around, and things look the same here, but yet it is all new."

"The Lord has blessed you," Sean told him, smiling, "You, and others here. This can be a new beginning, Degan."

It was nearly dark by the time they arrived back at Adolphustown, and as the canoes neared the shore, Sean could make out the figures of onlookers scattered here and there near the church. It occurred to him that it must be quite a spectacle, seeing the canoes returning, the tall Mohawk torches rising up above them to guide the way.

Charlotte and Abigail were not at the shore to greet him, and Sean decided it was due to the late hour. By now Abigail might be asleep. But upon opening the door he was pleased to find Charlotte just finishing setting two china plates on their small table, now covered with a dainty lace cloth. Glancing around the room he saw their delicate oil lamp burning reassuringly in the corner, casting a warm, cozy glow throughout the room. There were familiar pictures on the walls, and a fresh bed rug on Abigail's mattress, though their daughter was not present.

Charlotte moved to him, wrapping her arms around his neck, and Sean gladly embraced her. "You must be tired," she guessed, "How did the Mohawks receive you?"

"I think we shall see some of them at meeting house next Sunday," he nodded, then glanced again over toward Abigail's mattress. "Where is our daughter at this late hour?" he wondered.

"Abigail is staying at the Hollister's tonight," Charlotte smiled.

Sean slid his hands around her waist and pulled her to him. "All night?" he wondered.

"Uh huh," she nodded, stretching up to kiss him.

He reached back and untied her hair ribbon, running his hands through her dark tresses as they fell in long, loose curls down her back.

"Do you not want supper?" Charlotte wondered coyly, and he

knew she had her answer when he leaned down and kissed her passionately.

Outside, Willem was just returning from retrieving his account ledger from the tavern. He walked past the Brody's shanty and paused near the slightly open window, hearing laughter from inside.

"Well glory be," he whispered under his breath, continuing on toward home, "Glory be."

CHAPTER EIGHT

Sean worked diligently on his sermon throughout the week. He visited the homes of the sick and the elderly. He prayed to God that his work would not be wasted, and on the Sunday morning next, he and his family walked to the meeting house with hope in their hearts.

"What if no one comes today, Mama?" Abigail ventured.

"We must have faith, Little Abigail," Charlotte soothed, leaning over to kiss her daughter lightly on the forehead.

As on the dark day that had brought trouble to the church, Charlotte swung around somewhat apprehensively when she heard footsteps at the back, but to her relief, it was Eliza in the doorway, carrying baby Gideon. She was surrounded by the younger children, all pushing in behind her, though the oldest two, Bram and Susannah, were missing. Upon seeing Abigail, Emma beamed and ran to sit beside her. Eliza and the remaining children quickly followed suit.

"Willem insisted he needed the older children's help today," Eliza apologized, glancing self-consciously at the empty benches.

"Thank you for coming," Charlotte smiled.

Margaret says her parents won't come because they're Quackers," Emma shouted.

"Quakers, Emma, Quakers!" Eliza jumped in nervously.

Sean stopped pacing and stared out one of the windows that overlooked the bay. "We have a congregation," he announced.

Charlotte rose up from her bench to see what he was looking at. "The Mohawks!" she gasped.

Eliza and the children ran to the windows and stared in amazement at the sight. A flotilla of birch bark canoes was making its way toward the shore.

"God is good," Sean breathed.

"A few Mohawks pass by on their way to the trading post, but I haven't seen a group this large since the hungry year," Eliza commented, "Rations ran out, the snows were deep. They came across on the ice, bringing venison and supplies. The whole settlement would have starved were it not for them."

The children ran outside, eager to welcome their visitors.

"Slow down, children!" Eliza half-scolded, but she and Charlotte hurried excitedly from the church as well, watching Sean as he helped pull Degan's canoe up onto the shore.

"It's good to see you, brother," Sean placed a hand on Degan's shoulder.

"Yes, we are brothers," Degan confirmed, "And friends."

Sean nodded, then took in the twenty or so natives who had joined Degan on the journey. "Let us go inside!" he suggested happily, "The Lord awaits!"

Ten minutes later, Sean stood at the lectern surveying his silent congregation. Glancing down, he saw a Mohawk man sitting near one of the windows, fascinated with a fly that buzzed angrily against the glass. Another sat holding a hymn book in front of his face, and Sean wondered if he were able to read what he was looking at. A woman sat cross-legged on the floor, her sleeping daughter resting comfortably in her lap. Charlotte and Eliza sat in a front bench with Emma and Abigail crushed between them, the four sandwiched in by two large native women, one at either end. None were complaining. All was well.

The door creaked open just as the sermon was about to begin, and Sean paused, waiting to see who might join them next. The portly man who entered was well-dressed in a summer jacket and matching trousers, and yet his high-end apparel could not hide every flaw. Buttons held on for dear life, struggling to hold his shiny waistcoat together. A gold pocket watch barely managed to stretch across his sagging stomach, his white shirt pulled tight around his girth. He slowly raised a handkerchief to wipe the film of sweat from his face as he approached, slightly out of breath, with the assistance of a beautifully carved mahogany cane. Sheriff Cain followed dutifully at his heels. When he arrived in front of Sean, he planted his cane loudly on the wood floor and announced, "Reverend Brody, I am Franklin Wycherley." He glanced around the room. I see you have...something of a congregation."

Charlotte could see the suspicion in her husband's eyes as he replied, "There is still much work to be done, sir, but every new venture must have a beginning."

Wycherley glanced over at the women, and Eliza instinctively wrapped a protective arm around Emma.

"In any case it seems as though your work so far has failed to convey the message you were hoping for," Wycherley remarked, "Unless you consider a church full of heathens acceptable."

Degan stood, frowning, and was about to take a step toward Wycherley, when Sean held up a hand to stop him. "Perhaps my message was intercepted and twisted to serve another's purpose," he suggested.

Charlotte gasped as Wycherley lifted his cane and leaned forward, almost poking it into Sean's chest, "I would be very careful about making hasty accusations in God's house, Reverend," Wycherley warned.

Sean reached out, taking hold of the cane and pushing it downward as he stepped toward Wycherley. Sheriff Cain moved forward in response. "Now how come the last preacher wasn't this much fun--"

"There are children present!" Charlotte shouted, jumping to her feet. "Please stop this!"

Sean immediately stepped back in acknowledgement of her plea, and Wycherley waved a chubby hand in the air to stop Cain's advance, "Let him alone," he ordered, "Even his wife knows better than he does." He stared up at Sean and added, "She understands that any preacher who cares for the welfare of his congregation will not make trouble for me." He glanced over at Charlotte. "Don't you, Mrs. Brody?"

Charlotte did not answer. She glanced helplessly toward Sean, wishing he could do something, yet knowing he could not. She knew that he was fighting very hard to resist the urge to toss both Wycherley and Cain out of the church and into a heap on the ground, and she prayed he would be able to overcome the temptation.

"I wonder, Mr. Wycherley, do other judges have a sheriff working at their personal command?" Sean asked.

Wycherley huffed and wiped away more sweat from his forehead, ignoring Sean's inference, "I see you have two very fine horses tethered at your shanty, Reverend."

"Do my horses present a problem for you?" Sean asked.

Wycherley chuckled, shrugging. "It is only that I was surprised to think that you might be riding such fine horses, and two of them at that, when the Lord himself was content with nothing more than an ass."

Sean nodded. "Well, sir, it was impossible to find an ass in the vicinity, seeing as they've all been turned into judges."

Eliza let out a loud gasp, and Charlotte pressed a hand to her mouth to stifle her laughter.

Wycherley frowned and glared at Sean. "You'll see these pews filling up when the repairs have been paid for," he suggested, "And not before."

He turned and made his way toward the door. Cain offered Sean a long, smug grin, then followed after.

"Good day, Mrs. Hollister," Wycherley called out as he left, and Eliza sucked in a horrified breath. Charlotte knew the reason behind her concern. Wycherley was not offering a pleasant goodbye. He was letting Eliza know that he had seen her there, supporting the new church and the new preacher. Only God knew what that might mean for Willem or any of the Hollisters.

*****

It was usually Sean's snoring that woke Charlotte in the middle of the night, but in this instance she assumed it was the noticeable silence in the shanty as she opened her eyes slightly and rolled over, discovering that he was gone. The previous Sunday's events had upset him. She knew there was nothing she could say to make things better. He needed time to think, that was all.

Pushing herself up off the bed, she strained her eyes in the darkness, looking over to where Abigail lay sleeping soundly on her mattress. Sean would find a way through his troubles with Judge Wycherley, Charlotte thought to herself. For now, there was nothing that could be done, and she dropped her head back down onto the bed and drifted off again.

Sean wished he could sleep as peacefully as his wife and daughter. Walking alone along the shore of the bay seemed to be the only thing that could calm his restlessness. He loved the absolute quiet at this time of night, when even the birds were silently tucked away, their normally ceaseless chatter quelled.

And so it was that he was surprised to hear whispers in the darkness, the voices gradually growing louder and more agitated. When he clearly identified one of the voices as Caroline Wycherley's, he picked up the pace.

He saw them at the water's edge, Sheriff Cain with his arms wrapped tightly around her. It was clear that she could not pull away, though she was fighting him as best she could. Caroline lashed out, attempting to strike the Sheriff, but he responded by moving a hand to her bodice, beginning to tug at the strings on her dress.

"Cain!" Sean shouted, running toward them. It was enough to distract the Sheriff, allowing Caroline a moment to pull free of him. Cain drew his pistol, but at that moment, Sean raised his arm and instinctively threw a punch, hitting Cain in the head. He staggered back, dazed, falling backward as his pistol dropped to the ground.

Caroline moved quickly to take shelter behind Sean, and he motioned for her to remain a safe distance back while he cautiously approached a still-conscious Cain and picked up the pistol, leaning down to offer him a hand. Dazed, Cain accepted the help, and when he was finally back on his feet, his eyes widened with shock when Sean landed a blow to his left cheek that sent him flying back down onto the clay shore once again.

When Sean turned back to Caroline, her eyes were filled with tears, and she was desperately pulling at the front of her ripped, dirty dress in an attempt to salvage the damage.

"Miss Wycherley--" he began, but she glanced at him self-consciously and covered herself with her arms before turning and running off into the night.

"Wait!" he called after her, but Caroline quickly disappeared into the darkness.

Cain started to come around, groaning in pain. "You think Caroline is a good girl because she looks like an angel," Cain mumbled, "But she ain't no angel!"

Sean threw the pistol a safe distance away. "Something tells me you are not well qualified to speak on the subject of angels, Mr. Cain."

*****

Charlotte had spent the better part of the morning scrubbing clothes outside in the old wash bucket Eliza had given her. Sean had been awake early as usual, books laid out in front of him on the table as he read by the light of a small lamp. This was long before the first signs of any sunrise had begun to peek through the small window, and Charlotte remembered lifting her head from the pillow to glance at him. Reassured that he was home, she went back to sleep, not realizing until she woke later that she hadn't even heard him come in during the night. He would have entered quietly, to be sure, but she wondered if she should be taking a little more of Betsey's elixir to help with her fatigue. It was not in her nature to sleep so soundly, and it worried her to think of what might happen if Abigail were to wake in the night and need something in the darkness of the shanty.

Her back beginning to ache from bending over the bucket, Charlotte straightened up and glanced around the settlement. The sun was shining, but the wind had picked up a little and the bay was choppy. She walked a few steps, stopped, and turned back to look at the tiny wooden shack that had become her home. She thought back to all the nights she'd curled up atop her huge bed with Janey at the Hale residence. They'd chatter long into the night until finally her father would have to come to the door and remind them that there were others sleeping in the house. As different as their lives had been, she and Janey had always dreamed of the same future, a good husband and many children. But this, she had never counted on. It had never occurred to her that a life in the wilderness might be part of the bargain, but she was Sean's wife, and she had known when she'd married him that he was devoted to his work. She would continue to make the best of it, and she did believe that one day soon there would be a reward for her husband's hard work.

The door opened and Sean stepped out, bleary-eyed. His wavy dark brown hair was messed about and in need of a good chopping, Charlotte thought to herself. "You should sleep, darling," she suggested.

He shook his head, "There is much to do. I must get to meeting house."

"Why can't you simply continue to work here this morning?" she asked, "I will make you breakfast."

He shook his head, "I will come back for tea this afternoon." He glanced around, a little dazed, "I've forgotten my books," he realized.

"Wait here," she stopped him, turning and hurrying inside the shanty to the table where Sean's books sat waiting. Returning, she handed them to him, along with a small cloth bag. "Carraway cookies," she explained, "They will at least be something." She nodded in the direction of the church. "You have important work to do, Mr. Brody," she reminded him, "If you will not take my advice and rest, then you might as well be on your way."

He tucked the books under his arm and leaned forward, kissing her on the forehead. "Thank you," he whispered.

As he walked away, he glanced back and smiled when he saw Abigail bounding out of the shanty to help her mother with chores. Charlotte noticed him looking and offered a wave as she set about her tasks, as busy answering Abigail's multitude of questions as she was with putting out the wash.

"May I play at the shore today, Mama?" Abigail begged.

Charlotte glanced off in the direction of the bay, spying the whitecaps. "Perhaps another day, darling," she soothed.

"Oh please, Mama!"

Charlotte shook her head. "Abigail, if you ask again I'll have you peeling potatoes--"

"I'll be good, Mama!" Abigail interrupted, and Sean grinned, knowing that the mere mention of extra chores would be enough to keep their daughter mindful for the rest of the day.

Arriving at the church, he was surprised to discover Caroline sitting in one of the pews. She turned when she saw him, her face streaked with tears. "Reverend Brody," she sobbed, "I am so glad you're here."

CHAPTER NINE

Charlotte reached up to the clothesline and caught onto Abigail's dress as it flapped about in the wind. It was almost dry, as were most of the other clothes. Abigail had run off to play with Emma, and so with everything attended to, Charlotte decided to pack up the last piece of pigeon pie from last night's supper for Sean. She would take it to the church, and perhaps they could steal a few quiet minutes alone together.

She walked happily along the path to the meeting house, a small basket in hand. The winds pulled at her skirts, but the day was mild, and she was looking forward to surprising Sean. There was a slight sick feeling in her stomach which she blamed on her homesickness for Vermont. She would try to ignore it as she always did. Worrying over something she could not change was a waste of her energies. She needed to focus on working diligently to ensure that her marriage was growing stronger in spite of the challenges that she and Sean faced in this trying place.

Approaching the church, she saw that the door was open, so she stepped inside, expecting to find Sean sitting at the small desk he kept near the lectern for purposes of preparing his sermons. Instead, Charlotte heard hushed voices, deep in conversation. Not wanting to interrupt, she slowed her steps, stopping to peer around the corner from the small entranceway into the main part of the church. Sean was sitting on a bench with a woman whose long blonde hair fell loosely down her delicate shoulders and back. Charlotte let out a surprised gasp, leading Sean to leap to his feet and swing around to face her.

"Charlotte!" he exclaimed, "I did not expect you!"

"Yes," she replied, walking toward them and trying to conceal her jealousy, "So I see."

The woman stood and turned around, tears streaming down her face. Charlotte stopped her approach and instantly felt the heat of shame, "I am sorry," she blurted out, "I didn't not realize--"

The woman clasped a hand over her mouth to stifle her sobs and fled from the meeting house.

"Carolyn!" Sean shouted after her, "Wait!"

Charlotte felt another flash of panic. "Whatever is happening,

Sean? Please explain quickly so that we might go after that poor woman and offer her solace."

Sean waved a dismissive hand in the air and started away toward the door, "It is confidential," he told her.

Charlotte's eyes widened as she followed behind, "I come upon my husband in private counsel with a beautiful young woman, and I am not to ask questions?"

Sean swung around to face her. "I am her preacher, Charlotte. It is my duty to be present for the members of my congregation when they are in need--"

"And what exactly are that woman's needs, Mr. Brody?" Charlotte shot back, "Besides, I have not once seen her at meeting house before now. How do you claim her as a member of your flock?"

They stared at each other in silence, neither knowing what to say or how this might end, until Charlotte decided to finish it. "I will not allow this place to destroy what we have built as husband and wife, Sean," she announced, "I will go see to her."

"She is Caroline Wycherley," Sean nodded, "Judge Wycherley's daughter. Trouble follows her."

Charlotte brushed past him, leaving the church, and she did not feel him following behind her. As she stepped out, she saw the young woman standing near the water's edge, staring out at the bay. When she saw Charlotte approaching, she turned and quickly vanished into the nearby woods. Undeterred, Charlotte followed and discovered Caroline in a small, peaceful clearing. The sun streamed down in slivers from above the tops of the trees surrounding them.

"Is there anything I can do, Miss Wycherley?" Charlotte asked softly.

Caroline put a hand to her mouth, then hunched over, retching, and Charlotte hurried to pull her long hair back from her face, placing a reassuring hand on her shoulder until the worst had passed. Wiping her mouth with her sleeve, Caroline slowly straightened up and turned to Charlotte, her eyes swollen from crying. "There is nothing between your husband and me. He was merely offering comfort. Being that he's a man, he might not have told you that."

Charlotte nodded. "He told me nothing, so thank you for doing so. You must sit. Come."

She helped Caroline navigate over a soft bed of rotting leaves toward a tall tree that had fallen, and they sat together on it. "You are sick," Charlotte surmised, "We must find a doctor."

Caroline let out a half-hearted laugh. "No doctor can cure this sickness, Mrs. Brody. It's a midwife I'll be needing."

Charlotte's eyes grew wide with realization. "You're with child?"

Caroline sniffed and wiped more tears from her eyes.

"This news will not be welcomed by your family?" Charlotte asked tentatively.

Caroline almost snorted a laugh in reply, "What do you think?" she asked, "The only family I have is Judge Franklin Wycherley and I am an unmarried woman."

"Oh," Charlotte dropped her eyes, then slowly raised her head again to look at Caroline. "Who...is the father?"

Caroline shook her head. "That's the worse news yet, Mrs. Brody," adding quickly, "And it's not your husband."

"I did not suspect my husband," Charlotte shook her head, "But who is it?"

"The last man on earth my father would approve of," Caroline replied, and she turned to look at Charlotte, "Degan Hawke."

Charlotte felt her jaw drop open after this admission, but it could not be helped. "You...you--"

"I was with him yes," Caroline blurted out, "More than once."

Charlotte did not know how to respond. "Does...he know?" she wondered, "About the child?"

Caroline shook her head. "No one does, except for your husband and now you. But I can't hide it much longer." She reached down and touched her belly, and as the folds of her dress pulled tighter, Charlotte could clearly see the roundness. "Sheriff Cain already saw the bump. He was hidden in the woods, keeping watch on me as I swam." Caroline shivered as if thinking back on it.

"Will he tell your father?" Charlotte asked.

"Yes," Caroline replied, "He tells my father everything."

"Then you must seek out Mr. Hawke immediately," Charlotte advised, clasping her free hand over Caroline's, "You must tell him so that he can help you through this."

"You don't understand," Caroline explained, "My father will never allow me to give birth to Degan's child. Because of who he is. Because of where he comes from."

"He has a right to know," Charlotte reminded her, "Even if--" her voice trailed off.

"He's an Indian?" Caroline finished for her unapologetically.

"Mr. Hawke is Sean's friend. He returned our wagon. I know he is a good man," Charlotte smiled. She sat up straight and put an arm around Caroline's shoulders. "You already carry the child. Your father cannot stop it--"

"There are ways," Caroline cut her off and glanced out apprehensively toward the bay.

Horror swept through Charlotte. "No!" she protested, "No, God will not allow it!"

"My father is God in this town, Mrs. Brody," Caroline nodded, "If he wants this baby gone, no one will stop him."

Charlotte was about to suggest that they walk to the shanty to continue their discussion, when a shriek rose up in the air.

"Mrs. Brody!" Emma screamed from somewhere in the direction of the church, "Mr. Brody! Someone help! Someone help Abigail!"

*****

Sean bolted from the church upon hearing the screams and saw Emma running toward him.

"Abigail's in the bay!"

Sean looked off where Emma was pointing and saw Abigail struggling in the water. The wind and waves pushing her under each time she was able to surface.

"Sean!" Charlotte screamed, running toward the shore, but he reached it before she did and plunged into the water. He focused on Abigail, praying that each time she went under, she would reappear. He had almost reached her when she vanished completely.

"Abigail!" he heard Charlotte scream from somewhere behind him, and he took a deep breath, diving beneath the waves.

Sean tried desperately to adjust his eyes in the murky water, fighting through long, stringy weeds as he flailed for something, anything. She must be here somewhere.

Panic overcame him. He felt his heart pounding in his chest. It was all he could hear, thudding like a hollow drum. He didn't know what to do.

Then, in the midst of it all, a voice called out to him. It was not Charlotte. It was not their daughter. It spoke to him from some faraway place, and it told him to stop. To stop fighting. Stop moving. Just stop, and listen. His breath was almost gone, but he listened to the voice. He stayed beneath the waves. He closed his eyes. He listened. And in the silence, he heard something. Movement. Gurgling. Struggling.

Sean opened his eyes, and there in front of him was his Little Abigail, floating lifelessly just beneath the surface, her arms dangling out in front of her. Instantly, Sean propelled himself forward and grabbed her around the waist.

The silence was replaced with Charlotte's screams when he resurfaced, pulling Abigail toward the shore. By now there was a small crowd of concerned onlookers gathered near Charlotte, and Eliza was there, holding her. The two women ran to Sean as he lifted Abigail out of the water and placed her down onto the clay shore.

"She was trying to swim with a kite as Reverend Brody had done," Emma sputtered, half-crying as she grabbed on to her mother's arm.

"Do something Sean! Charlotte wailed, dropping down at their daughter's side.

"Dear God," Sean prayed, and leaning over Abigail, he gazed down into her beautiful face, her eyes closed peacefully, "Please save her. Do not take her from us, Lord!"

"Someone please help!" Charlotte cried, "Prayer is not enough, Sean! It is not enough!" Sobbing, she reached out and took Abigail's shoulders in her hands and started to shake her.

"Stop!" The woman's voice was firm, authoritative, and Charlotte recognized it immediately.

Betsey Braswell stepped from the crowd. "Put her hands over her head!"

Charlotte moved quickly and did as she asked without question. "What next?" she demanded, "Quickly!"

"Charlotte--" Sean began, uncertain.

"The water must come out," Betsey replied, and she dropped down onto her knees beside Abigail and began to push on her chest.

"What are you doing?" Sean panicked.

Charlotte watched Abigail's face and thought she saw a change. She raised a hand in the air toward Sean, "Let her continue," she nodded.

"God bless this child," Betsey Braswell chanted with each push, "God bless this child, God bless this child."

Sean's eyes changed from fear to hope when he saw Abigail's lips quiver. "Little Abigail!" he called out, "Please come back to us!"

Charlotte wrapped her arms around herself and rocked back and forth on her knees, crying, "God bless this child," she whispered along with Betsey, "God bless this child."

Betsey stopped chanting. She looked down at Abigail's face and pressed hard on her chest once more. The crowd around them was silent, with only the sound of the waves washing up on shore as a backdrop to the fear.

Water gushed from Abigail's mouth, then more, and still more until finally Betsey leaned forward and took the girl's head in her hands, sitting her up. Abigail's eyes shuddered open, and she began to cry. "Mama! Papa?"

"Abigail!" Charlotte cried, throwing her arms around her daughter.

Sean smiled, then felt his hands begin to shake. It was the relief of it all, he thought to himself. The trembling ran up his arms, along his back, and through his legs. He finally exhaled, not sure he remembered when he had last taken in a breath. His wet hair dripped wet onto the clay shore.

"You are in shock," Betsey said, watching him, "Go home with your family and rest. Your wife can give you something to calm your nerves."

Sean glanced, bewildered, at Charlotte, but she quickly changed the subject.

"Let's get Little Abigail home," she urged.

Betsey stood up, stepping back, and the villagers moved away from her in trepidation.

"Thank you!" Charlotte gushed, pulling Abigail's wet hair

back from her face, "Thank you ever so much, Mrs. Braswell!"

Sean leaned forward and kissed Abigail on the cheek, then found the strength to rise on his weakened legs. "May God bless you," he nodded to Betsey.

Except for her brief exchange with Charlotte, her face had seemed hard, her eyes without emotion, but now she softened and smiled at Sean, then turned and slowly disappeared along the path that led back up to the church.

Sean fell back to his knees and gathered Abigail up into his arms. He pulled her close, and when Charlotte had risen and taken his arm, they walked back to the shanty in silence.

The following morning, concerned settlers were huddled outside the Brody's shanty, quietly chatting. When the door finally opened, Charlotte stepped out, followed by a somber Sean.
Emma came running toward them and threw her arms around Charlotte's waist. "Mrs. Brody, how is Abigail?"

"She's sleeping now, Emma," Charlotte soothed, running a hand through the girl's hair, "She had a terrible fright, but she will be fine."

Sean turned to address the expectant crowd. "Thank you all so much for your concern," he announced, his deep voice booming across the settlement, "Our daughter is resting comfortably now."

Satisfied that Abigail was recovering, the people began slowly making their way back to their homes and chores, and Charlotte turned and disappeared back inside the shanty.

Willem approached and offered Sean a pat on the back, then took Emma's hand and began to lead her away toward their cabin.

"Will," Sean called out, "The woman who saved Abigail – who is she?"

Willem ushered Emma off inside the cabin before turning back to Sean. "That's Calvin Braswell's wife. They say she's a witch, if you believe in such things."

CHAPTER TEN

"You know the witch." It was late evening and quiet in the shanty. Abigail was resting, but Charlotte glanced over to the mattress to ensure that their daughter was sound asleep before turning back to Sean across the table. She had expected that this conversation would arise, and she set down the book she'd been reading as she gathered her thoughts.

"You wanted me to visit every cabin and I did," she shrugged, keeping her voice low, "Besides, she is a woman, like me and Eliza. She is not a witch."

"But she is not like you and Eliza," Sean shook his head, "She brews potions and does not attend church."

"That does not make her a witch," Charlotte shot back, checking again to be sure that Abigail was still sleeping. "Besides," she added, "Mrs. Braswell saved Abigail's life! She deserves our respect and our friendship. As Adolphustown's preacher, you should not breed such false ideas."

Sean hesitated, then nodded. "Perhaps you are correct," he acknowledged, "It is true that I have never seen a witch, as far as I know."

"People fear what they do not understand, Sean," Charlotte reminded him, "Some have feared you in the past because of your size. They do not take the time to know you. This is something that has always frustrated you, my darling. Imagine what Betsey and Calvin Braswell must face every day here in their own community."

He nodded and let out a breath. "It seems I still have much to learn, Mrs. Brody."

"We are learning together, Sean," she nodded, "You are a leader in the Fourth. You can use that influence to help others move past their own ignorance and build a better home for all of us. That is why we are here, isn't it?"

Sean reached across the table and took her hands in his, "It is sometimes easy to forget why we are here," he admitted softly, "Which is why I am so grateful that you are always here to remind me."

*****

Charlotte was amazed at Abigail's speedy recovery, and she was soon able to dedicate herself once again to helping Sean grow his congregation. Each Sunday they saw a few more settlers ignore the threats of Franklin Wycherley as they turned up in clean church clothes, their children's faces freshly scrubbed. Though the number of Mohawks who made the trip across the bay began to dwindle, Degan Hawke was always in attendance, and Charlotte had to wonder if it wasn't because he was hoping to catch a glimpse of Caroline Wycherley. She was now rarely seen in Adolphustown, though her pregnancy was the talk of the settlement. Charlotte thought of her often, and on one particularly fine early summer day, she decided to visit.

"Is Miss Wycherley about?" she asked the timid young servant girl who opened the door. Her black hair was a mass of tight, frizzy curls, and her lovely dark skin was flawless thanks to her youth. Charlotte glanced at her drab brown dress, set off by the clean white apron that covered it.

"She don't see nobody these days," the girl said quietly.

"Oh, but, perhaps if you told her it is Mrs. Brody she might change her mind," Charlotte suggested.

"It's alright, Lucy," Caroline's voice drifted to the door from somewhere down the hallway, "Please see Mrs. Brody in."

Lucy led Charlotte to the parlour, brought a tea tray, and quickly disappeared.

"She is a servant, yet she is also my friend," Caroline explained, entering the room. Her pregnancy was glaringly obvious now, impossible to hide even with full skirts.

"I have known a similar friendship," Charlotte confessed, thinking of dear Janey. "How are you feeling?"

Caroline slowly lowered herself down into the wing chair across from Charlotte. "Like a cow," she admitted, grinning.

"And so I assume that your father has accepted your pregnancy?" Charlotte asked, leaning forward to pour two cups of tea.

"With one condition," Caroline nodded, picking up her tea cup and taking a sip. "I must marry him and tell people that the baby is his."

"What?" Charlotte nearly dropped her cup. She set it down

onto the tray on the table between them and looked to Caroline for some explanation.

"There is something you do not know, Mrs. Brody," Caroline told her, "Franklin Wycherley is not my father. He met and married my mother several years ago."

Charlotte gasped. "Where is your mother now?"

"Gone," Caroline half-whispered, and Charlotte heard the pain in the young woman's voice, "He told me she ran off with another man."

"Do you believe that?" Charlotte pressed.

Caroline paused, then said, "It does not matter what I believe, Mrs. Brody. My mother is gone, and all I have left is him. If I try to leave, there will be consequences."

"But now you have Degan!" Charlotte exclaimed.

"I have not seen him in many weeks," Caroline explained, "And if I cross Wycherley, he will banish me from this place, or worse. I must think of my child."

"Did you reveal to him who the father is?"

Caroline shook her head, "I did not have to. He was already suspicious. Sheriff Cain had seen me with Degan in the woods on occasion."

"But what if the baby looks like Degan? The secret will be revealed and then Heaven knows what trouble may come upon you and the child. Miss Wycherley, you must tell Mr. Hawke!" Charlotte urged.

Caroline shook her head. "I have not seen him since the day he returned your wagon, and Cain watches everything I do. There is no way for me to contact him, and I am hardly in any state to canoe across the bay on my own."

"He is at meeting house every Sunday," Charlotte informed her.

"Wycherley will not allow me to be seen until after the baby is born," Caroline protested softly, "Besides, what would I tell Degan? That I am having his child, and it will be raised by another man? My own father?" She turned away, a look of disgust crossing her face.

"When we think there is only one path, there is always another," Charlotte insisted, "If I could find a way to reunite you with Mr. Hawke, would you want that?"

Caroline nodded, her eyes filling with tears, "Oh, yes, Mrs. Brody, I have thought of no one but him for weeks. My heart aches for Degan, and I beg you to tell no one, not even your husband, of my father's awful plan. I would not want my love to hear it through exaggerated gossip. And if word gets out before he is ready to announce it his way, he will know that I imparted the information, and he will find a way to punish me."

"I am shocked that you are capable of calling him your father at all," Charlotte admitted.

"Mrs. Brody!" Franklin Wycherley's shrill voice rang out from the parlour doorway. "My daughter didn't tell me we were expecting company."

Charlotte exchanged a worried glance with Caroline, wondering if the judge might have overheard their conversation. "I only dropped in to see how your daughter is feeling," Charlotte said, and rising from her chair, she picked up her tea and quickly took a polite sip, setting the cup back on the tray when she was done. "It was good to see you, Caroline," she nodded, "Please do let me know if there is anything you need."

"Thank you, Mrs. Brody," Caroline smiled, dabbing at her eyes with a handkerchief. She glanced at Wycherley, his gaze weighing heavily on her, "But my father is taking good care of me," she finished.

Charlotte knew that she was lying. "And so he should," she answered, turning to glare at the judge.

He fired back with a scornful look, but Charlotte felt satisfied that she had made her point.

Leaving the grand house, she began to make her way back toward the shanty, and just within sight of the Hollister's cabin, she had the overwhelming feeling that she were being watched. Stopping, she turned back toward the woods.

"Hello?" she called out nervously, "Is anyone there?"

When there was no immediate response, Charlotte decided she would rather not stay to wait for one, and swinging around again, she nearly jumped out of her skin when she ran headlong into Solomon Roberts. She and Sean had joined his family for supper and fellowship one recent evening, and she had been impressed with the well-built teenager's mature demeanor. He was their only child, and looked much like his father, John, with a freckled face, tousled, shoulder-length auburn hair, and a moustache to match. It also didn't go unnoticed by Charlotte that Solomon's broad shoulders and muscular arms came close to rivalling those of her own husband.

"Excuse me, Mrs. Brody," Solomon apologized, quickly removing his hat and almost dropping it in the process.

"Mr. Roberts, you nearly frightened the life out of me!" Charlotte responded, clasping a hand to her chest.

"I'm just heading down to the bay for a swim, Mrs. Brody," Solomon explained, "My chores are done, and a swim always cools me off."

Charlotte glanced back at the bay. "You Upper Canadians are a hardy lot," she admitted, "It's already July and the bay is still not quite temperate enough for my liking. I'm not sure that it shall ever be."

Solomon chuckled timidly until some sobering thought must have crossed his mind, for his eyes turned serious. "How is your daughter doing, Mrs. Brody? I was sorry to hear of her accident."

Charlotte nodded. "She is getting better every day, and when the water does warm, I do plan to teach her to swim in the bay. I don't want her to be afraid of it, especially after what happened. There was a time when I enjoyed regular visits to the beach near my home in Vermont," she reflected wistfully.

"I'm envious," he admitted, "I've seen naught but this bay and its shores. But I would wager that any place with your seal of approval would have a special place in any man's heart, Mrs. Brody."

Charlotte felt her face flush with heat, and she suddenly felt uncomfortable being alone with the young man in such an isolated spot. "It is getting late, Mr. Roberts," she told him, "My husband waits for me."

"Of course, ma'am," he agreed, proceeding to awkwardly replace his hat as Charlotte began to move off toward the shanty.
"What was that?" he piped up suddenly, and Charlotte turned back to him.

"I heard nothing," she replied.

Solomon looked off into the forest. "I think there's someone in there. It could be Mohawks."

Charlotte thought of Degan. Perhaps he was waiting close by, hoping to catch a glimpse of Caroline. "If so, I am certain that they mean no harm, Mr. Roberts," she said, "It's best to leave well enough alone."

"I'll be fine, Mrs. Brody," he assured her bravely as he moved toward the forest path, "Could just be an animal. Either way, I'll take care of things, don't you worry."

Charlotte took a deep breath and watched as he headed off into the trees, disappearing into the thick brush. She waited, hoping there would be no trouble.

"Mr. Roberts?" she called out after a minute or two of silence, "Solomon?"

Alarmed when there was no response, she turned and hurried to fetch help. "I fear he may be in some predicament," she worried aloud, returning with Willem at her side.

"Probably nothing," he shrugged, gazing off into the trees, "Anyway, that young Roberts lad is strong as an ox."

"No doubt," Charlotte agreed. "Still, I would feel somewhat more relieved if we could ensure that all is well."

Willem let out a sigh. "You women worry too much, but I will have a look to relieve your mind."

Charlotte's concern for Solomon Roberts was far greater than any worries she had about imposing on Willem, and she showed him the place where the young man had disappeared from view. He was out of sight for only a short time before he reappeared, walking briskly toward her, his face filled with concern.

Charlotte's heart began to pound. "What is it?"

"Get Sean," Willem instructed, "Tell him to come quick."

*****

Sean removed his hat to knock upon John Roberts' door, and when it opened, he immediately saw the distress upon the man's face. He held out his hand in friendship. "Mr. Roberts, my prayers are with your son. How is he?"

John shook his head. "He took quite a knocking, and is still abed. He can't open his eyes. We've tried to bathe the blood away, but there are so many wounds--" his words trailed off and he nodded, unable to finish.

"Would you like me to see him?" Sean wondered.

98

"His mother's in a terrible state," John answered, shaking his head, "She won't leave his side, and she'll barely let me in the room. Perhaps in a few days, Reverend."

"Does he know who did this?" Sean asked.

"He can hardly speak. All I got out of him so far is that something hit him. Says it felt like an entire tree got him square in the back of the head. The rest," John paused, looking down at his shoes, "The rest must have been done to him after he was down. They left him for dead, by the looks of it."

Sean twisted his hat in his hands. It concerned him to think that there was someone in or near Adolphustown who could cause such harm to one of their own. "Willem tells me you have sent for a doctor, but it may be tomorrow or the next day before he arrives. In the meantime, Mr. Roberts, I wondered if you might consider asking Mrs. Braswell to--"

John shook his head. "My wife was there to see what happened with your daughter, and she wanted to call for Mrs. Braswell, but I'm not inclined to agree. I don't want any of that witchery in my home. Some say she's a healer, but only God heals, isn't that right, Mr. Brody?"

Sean thought for a moment. "I believe that God heals through the work of caring hands, Mr. Roberts. You must make the decision that you think is best, but I will tell you that it was Mrs. Braswell's hands that saved my daughter's life. God was there through her."

"I won't be allowing that woman anywhere near my home just the same," John insisted, "Solomon is a strong lad. He'll have to get through it on his own."

"He is strong," Sean agreed, "Which leads me to wonder if there may have been more than one man involved in the attack."

"Did they teach you to be a lawman at those church schools you went to, Preacher?" Sheriff Cain stood watching them from a short distance away, "'Cause we don't need no more lawmen around here."

"I must disagree," Sean countered, turning to face him, "If you cannot apprehend those responsible for the attack on Solomon Roberts, perhaps the people of Adolphustown do need a new sheriff."

"And what do you think, Mr. Roberts?" Cain wondered, staring past Sean to where John stood in the doorway, "Do you blame your sheriff for what happened to your boy?"

Sean turned back and saw John's face harden as he glared at Cain, "I think I hear Agnes calling." He looked at Sean and nodded, "Thank you for your concern, Reverend."

When he had closed the door, Sean turned and pulled his hat on, brushing past Cain as he set out for the church. "If you will excuse me, Sheriff, some people in this settlement have important work to do."

CHAPTER ELEVEN

"Are you happy, Mrs. Brody?" Sean asked the question as he sat at the table and gazed across the room. Charlotte was near the window, immersed in a letter she was reading while standing in a flood of midsummer sunlight.

She glanced up and shrugged. "Of course I am happy, Sean," she answered, "And I shall remain so as long as I have you and Abigail."

He nodded, but somehow he didn't feel completely convinced. "How is Janey doing?" he asked.

Charlotte sighed. "I cannot believe I am admitting it, but I am pleased to hear that she and Daniel are enjoying one another's company."

Sean smiled. "Hmmm...perhaps Daniel finally recognizes the benefits of a settled life."

"Perhaps," Charlotte shrugged, "That, or he finally sees what has been there in front of him all along. He escorted her to a spring frolic, and she wore a dress I'd given her. I'm sure she looked lovely."

Sean thought for a moment. "You miss those frolics, don't you?"

Charlotte shook her head. "I do not think it is the parties I miss quite so much as the people...and the music. You know how my father liked to invite musicians to the house to entertain our guests." She glanced out the window, "It is so quiet here."

"We have our hymns on Sundays," he reminded her.

"It is not the same," she shook her head, turning back to him.

"Unfortunately there is only so much I can offer you here, Charlotte. Perhaps, when I receive my posting in England--"

"I am not asking you to give me anything more, Sean," she cut in, "I have told you that I am happy, as happy as might be expected given our situation. If I seem preoccupied, it is only that I have just received this bittersweet letter from Janey. I love hearing her news, but I am heavy-hearted when the most I have to offer in reply is to tell her that our little Abigail almost drowned this summer, and a young man was nearly killed in the woods."

Sean exhaled loudly and took a sip of his tea, "I admit it has been a difficult time," he nodded, "But it has only been a little over two months and already the congregation is growing, in spite of Franklin Wycherley's efforts to stifle it. Bishop Weston will be impressed with my progress, Charlotte. Perhaps we will find ourselves posted to England well before the snow falls this winter."

Charlotte sighed, "I can only imagine that winter must be unbearable here," she answered, again glancing absently out the window, "The weakest part of me prays that we might leave by then."

"And the strongest part of you?" he wondered.

She smiled and looked at him, "When I am feeling strong I can admit to myself that we need to persevere."

Sean nodded. "You keep me on the path I need to walk, Mrs. Brody," he smiled, "I do not like to think what my life would be without you."

She went to him, planting a kiss upon his forehead before folding the letter and placing it in a small box she'd reserved for such things in a steamer trunk in the corner.

Sean turned back to the table in front of him and tried to focus on the book he'd been studying, but just as he regained his focus, he found himself distracted again by the sound of voices outside the shanty. Charlotte followed him as he went to investigate.

A group of curious settlers had gathered on the tavern steps and were eagerly discussing something that had caught their interest. Some were pushing forward to try to read a bill that had been posted on the door. Willem made his way down the steps, a look of concern on his face as he approached Sean and Charlotte.

"What is it, Will?" Sean wondered.

"It's trouble, that's what," Willem shook his head, "Wycherley's arranged the annual boxing match between Adolphustown and Marysburgh."

Abraham Thurlow stormed down the steps and joined them. "Wycherley knows very well we can't win this with Solomon Roberts still on the mend!"

"That's why he wants it now," Willem nodded, "He needs to win it. He's after something."

"Why a boxing match?" Sean asked.

"He sets one every year between Adolphustown and

Marysburgh," Willem explained, "It was all in good fun at the start, but every year the stakes grow bigger. Roberts is our strongest man, so now it's clear why he's been disabled."

"That attack was intentional," Sean concluded.

Willem nodded, "Wycherley has already determined the outcome of this match."

Sean looked surprised. "You do not strike me as the kind of man who gives up so easily, Will."

Willem crossed his arms in front of him, "You know we can't fight him, Sean. Wycherley owns this settlement."

"Expansion is the true mark of a man, Mr. Hollister," Judge Wycherley waddled into view, Sherriff Cain close behind. Any settlers still gathered in front of the tavern went scrambling back to their own affairs. "I am only expanding my worth as any man would do under the same circumstances," Wycherley shrugged.

"Most men in the Fourth seek only to take proper care of their families. What need is there beyond that?" Sean asked.

Wycherley approached the men and planted his cane firmly into the ground as if he planned to be there for a very long time. "Perhaps you could ask that question of the American Stephen Girard," he challenged, "He is one of the richest men in the world and has no family of his own, no children to leave it to."

"Then he is not a rich man," Sean suggested.

Wycherley glanced around him, then sighed, "Yes, I suppose wealth is truly a matter of one's perspective, Reverend Brody, but you see as much as I do try to expand productivity here, I must admit that even I sometimes wonder why I stay in this meager settlement, overflowing with broken-down shanties and a useless church."

"Then perhaps it's time to leave these people alone," Sean suggested.

"I would love to, Reverend Brody," Wycherley nodded, "But the people of Adolphustown must first pay their debts to me. I admit it is unfortunate that many of these good folk are working every day to try to regain something that may never be theirs again. It does seem quite pointless. However, any land deeded to me was traded fair and square and legally signed over." He paused, then continued, "But you know, the land can belong to them again, and your church to the Methodists, Mr. Brody. All losses can be made good if Adolphustown wins the boxing match against Marysburgh."

"You will erase all debts if Adolphustown wins?" Sean asked.

"Every one of them," Wycherley nodded, "And the same reward will be extended to the people of Marysburgh should their man be triumphant."

"And if we lose?" Willem ventured.

Wycherley spun his cane around in the soil. "Nothing need change immediately," he shrugged, "However, if Marysburgh wins I will naturally need to make up for my losses by initiating the sale of some of my properties here in the Fourth."

"You know we can't win it without Solomon Roberts," Willem raised his voice in frustration.

"Perhaps you can enter the ring, Mr. Hollister," Wycherley glanced at Willem, "I hear you have quite a temper - and fists to match." He craned his short neck to look up at Sean, "Or perhaps Mr. Brody will have a go at it," he suggested, "As long as God and his wife will allow him, that is."

Sean stepped confidently toward Wycherley, "You cannot bargain with people's homes and property through betting and speculation. This is unlawful activity--"

"And I am the local magistrate," the judge reminded him. "Those outside the Fourth Township have neither the time nor the energy to devote to weeding through our petty business here, Mr. Brody. As far as they are concerned, I have saved this struggling settlement time and again, and they are correct in their assumptions. I am only trying to help, Reverend," he finished, then lifted his cane and shook the dirt from its tip before he turned and walked away.

*****

Perhaps it was the heat of a summer's night, or perhaps there were simply too many thoughts racing through his head. Sean opened his eyes and slowly turned to look at Charlotte, her sleeping face bathed in moonlight glowing through the small window near their bed. He felt a twinge of envy watching her sleep, wishing he could rest as easily. He sat up quietly, though trying not to disturb her was not an easy thing, such was his size and weight. He paused for a moment as she stirred and rolled over, but she did not wake. Standing up, he looked over to the corner where Abigail lay on her mattress, though he already knew full well that she was safe in bed. Little Abigail could snore as loudly as any farmer in Adolphustown, Sean chuckled to himself.

It was then that he saw the flickering light through the window, and as with the first time he had seen it, that light was followed by another, and in a few moments, a third. He went to the door and opened it, looking down toward the shore of the bay. He waited, then saw another flame, and quickly realized that he was watching a parade of people carrying flaming torches as they made their way along the water's edge.

Closing the door quietly behind him, Sean proceeded along the path toward the church, keeping an eye on the torches as he walked. Seeing one person fall away from the group, he set out after them, following the flame to the Van Horn house. There he watched Walter Van Horn usher his wife and children inside before safely extinguishing his pine torch in a pile of dirt in the side yard.

"Mr. Van Horn!" Sean called out softly as he approached.

Walter swung around in surprise, "Reverend!"

"No one mentioned any community activities were scheduled for this evening," Sean said, "Or perhaps my wife and I were intentionally overlooked?"

Walter paused before he spoke. "I cannot lie to you, Reverend. It is true. You and Mrs. Brody were not invited for a reason."

Sean could not hide his bewilderment. "Should I be concerned, Mr. Van Horn?" he wondered, "Is there something wicked afoot in those woods?"

"Oh no, nothing wicked at all, Reverend," Walter assured him before adding, "Let me show you something."

Sean waited as Walter disappeared around the corner of the cabin and returned with a violin in one hand, a bow in the other.

"Do you play?" Sean asked.

"On occasion," Walter admitted, "Though Reverend Culpepper before you made it clear that I was to stop, as music is a snare of the devil."

Sean glanced at the violin in the moonlight. "So you hide this? The whole settlement hides it?"

"Only after you arrived," Walter admitted, "We did not think you would look happily upon it, and so once a week we travel to Samuel Braxton's for music and fellowship."

"Braxton," Sean recalled, "He is a bit of a hermit who lives a good stretch along the shore."

"He keeps to himself, but he loves music," Walter explained, "And he lives far enough away that we cannot be heard here in the settlement. I am awful sorry that we kept this from you, Reverend Brody. The deceit should lay squarely on my shoulders alone."

Sean shook his head. "An apology is not necessary, Mr. Van Horn," he shook his head, "I do wish you had come to me with this, however I also understand why you did not."

"I will dispose of it," Walter nodded, glancing down wistfully at his cherished violin, "As I promised Reverend Culpepper I would do."

"There is no need," Sean insisted—

"But music goes against your Methodist teachings," Walter reminded him.

Sean nodded. "Every Preacher must take his community into consideration, and every community is different, Mr. Van Horn. Besides, I do not believe the devil could reside within so beautiful an instrument."

"I agree," Walter replied, relief in his voice, "And yet I am surprised to hear you say it."

Sean nodded. "It is what my wife would say," he smiled, "And I have learned that it is best to always listen to my wife."

Walter grinned and nodded. "Then with your permission Reverend, we shall host our next evening of music here, in my home, and if you are willing, you and Mrs. Brody will be our special guests."

*****

The message was delivered by a young dark-skinned servant boy. He shrank back when Sean first opened the door, then reached into his pocket and produced a small note, which Sean accepted with a nod, "Thank you."

His task complete, the boy turned and ran, barefoot, back along the path that led down toward the bay, and in the direction of the

Wycherley house.

"You should not go," Charlotte warned Sean, busy with her needlework at the kitchen table, "Whatever would you need to speak with Judge Wycherley about?"

"I have no idea, which is why I must go," Sean explained, refolding the note and pulling on his hat.

"Perhaps Willem should accompany you," she suggested.

"There is no need to draw anyone else in until more has been revealed," he finished, and he leaned down and kissed her.

"Papa loves you, Mama!" Abigail squealed, looking up from her book as she lay on her mattress.

"Yes I do!" Sean proclaimed, kissing Charlotte again and prompting Abigail to playfully cover her eyes, giggling.

"I won't be long," he assured Charlotte, touching his hand to her cheek. She nodded and smiled.

"Be mindful of your mother!" he called out to Abigail before leaving them.

It was only a short walk to the Wycherley house, which was set in amongst the trees just at the edge of the forest, facing the settlement. Sean knocked, then turned and looked back over Adolphustown, noting that the judge was allowed a pleasing view of all of the various comings and goings from this location.

He was shown into the Wycherley study by a female servant, who bowed slightly to the preacher before promptly turning to leave, closing the heavy wooden door behind her.

Wycherley was sitting behind his desk and did not immediately look up from the parchment documents he was reading. Sean stood staring at the shelves of books that lined the walls as he waited for the judge to acknowledge his presence. He had no idea why he had been summoned, but he did not intend to stay any longer than was necessary.

Finally Wycherley raised a hand and motioned for Sean to sit in the chair on the opposite side of the huge desk, and he reluctantly plopped down as invited.

"I am impressed, Preacher," Wycherley spoke up, leaning back in his chair and lacing his fingers together across his round belly, "You came."

"Why am I here?" Sean demanded, "I have more important things to--"

The door opened behind him and he turned to see Caroline enter with a tea tray. He remembered Charlotte looking a similar size when she was far along in her pregnancy with Abigail, and so he guessed that Caroline might be due to have her baby soon.

"Reverend Brody," she smiled, then curtsied slowly and carefully before setting the tray on a tea table beside the desk. She stepped back and stood in front of the study window. The morning light framed her huge belly in a way that seemed somehow heavenly to Sean.

"Caroline and I are soon to be wed," Wycherley said.

Sean wasn't certain he'd heard the judge correctly, and he glanced up at Caroline, who quickly turned away. "I do not understand," he replied.

Wycherley laughed, "Well now, Reverend, I can imagine your shock, wondering how such a thing could be possible!" He stood and stepped close to Caroline, reaching out for her hand. She glanced sideways at Sean, unable to look him in the eye, and hesitantly offered her hand to Wycherley. When he took it, Sean was certain he saw her wince.

"She was my wife's daughter," Wycherley explained, "Not of my blood. And now that her mother has been gone for a sufficient time, the law says that Caroline is no longer my stepdaughter and so we may marry." He glanced at her, "Isn't that right, dear?"

Caroline pulled her hand away from his, "You know the law better than anyone," she suggested, folding her arms in front of her.

Sean felt sick for Caroline Wycherley. "And you have both agreed that this is best for everyone involved?" he wondered, "Including the infant?"

Wycherley returned to his chair, "The child will be born with a silver baby spoon in its mouth," he huffed, "Privileged like its mother, who came by her own good fortune through me as well."

"May I be excused?" Caroline interjected, "I am afraid that I am suddenly not feeling well." She offered Sean a look that told him she was not happy with the prospect of having to marry Franklin Wycherley.

"Go on, then," Wycherley grumbled, "Get out."

She hurried away, her head down, closing the door behind her.

"You should be ashamed," Sean scolded, "Any man in this

town, and certainly every woman would know that Caroline has no interest in marrying you. What of the baby's father?"

Wycherley frowned, "I am the father as far as the world should be concerned," he shot back, "And that harlot is fortunate to have any man look at her twice!"

"Even you?" Sean wondered.

Wycherley stared unhappily across the desk and let out a deep breath, "You seem quite concerned with my daughter's welfare, Mr. Brody--"

"She is not your daughter," Sean reminded him curtly.

"In any case," the judge continued unheeded, "You can choose to change the fate of everyone in Adolphustown, including Caroline. Their future can be in your hands, or should I say, your fists, Reverend Brody."

Sean furrowed his eyebrows, bewildered, though on some level he already suspected what would come next.

"I have been looking into your credentials," Wycherley continued. "Your banishment from New York must have been quite a shock to your wife, even more so when she discovered the reason behind it." He paused. "She does know about your nocturnal activities, doesn't she, Reverend?"

"What do you want?" Sean demanded.

"You have quite a reputation as a champion in stage boxing," Wycherley nodded, "Which could be quite profitable for our town."

"Profitable for the town magistrate, you mean," Sean corrected.

Wycherley shrugged. "The town's success is my success as well."

Sean stood up and turned to leave, stopping momentarily to announce, "I am a man of God. Fighting of any kind goes against my beliefs."

"What about your belief in the people of the Fourth Township?" Wycherley asked, "What about your belief in that little church down the path? Winning the match for Adolphustown would clear every debt owed me in the Fourth."

Sean turned back to Wycherley's desk.

"You also mentioned Caroline's fate," Sean reminded him.

"Oh, yes," Wycherley nodded, as if remembering something inconsequential, "If you fight and win, Caroline will not be forced to marry me." He paused before continuing, "Though if I do not support whomever she does eventually choose for a husband she will of course be turned out, and I will no longer be responsible for any of her troubles or debts."

Sean thought for a moment, then repeated, "I am a man of God," and he turned again, pulling his hat on as he stepped out into the hallway.

"Think on it!" he heard Wycherley call out, "You can change everything for these people, Reverend!"

*****

Charlotte was still working at needlepoint when Sean arrived home. The day had turned cloudy and so she had lit the lamp earlier than usual and was straining a little toward its light as she worked. She looked up when he entered. "The meal won't be long," she told him, "Bram Hollister brought fresh pigeon."

Sean nodded, more concerned with what was on his mind than what would soon be in his stomach.

"How is Caroline?" Charlotte asked, "Did you see her?"

"Yes," Sean answered, removing his hat and dropping it on the table, "She has grown much larger than when I saw her only last month."

"That was weeks ago," Charlotte smiled. "Babies grow a little bigger every day."

"Did you know about this strange marriage that Wycherley is forcing her into?" Sean asked.

Charlotte hesitated, then admitted, "She asked me not to mention it. I think she is ashamed."

"The shame is not hers to carry."

"I know that, Sean," Charlotte agreed, "But if she insists on going along with it, I am not sure if there is anything we can do. What did Judge Wycherley want to see you about?"

He removed his jacket and draped it over the back of a chair, then exhaled loudly as he sat down across from her. "This fight that he is staging can't be won by Adolphustown. It's impossible without Solomon Roberts."

Charlotte's needle froze mid-stitch. "I do not understand why a fight would be so important to anyone," she shook her head.

"I would agree in this case if it meant that the lives of all of our neighbours would not be affected."

Charlotte set her work on the table and looked across at him. "In what way?" she asked.

"Wycherley has cheated many of these people out of their properties. The deeds show that he owns most of Adolphustown, and dishonestly or otherwise, they'll be in his debt for years unless--"

"Unless they win a boxing match against Marysburgh," she finished for him.

"The Roberts boy was our best hope to win," he nodded.

"There is no one else?" she asked.

"Perhaps one other," he answered.

Her face turned grave and she pushed her chair out behind her to stand up. "You promised me you would never go back to it again," she reminded him, stepping away from the table.

"And I have not!" he assured her, rising to his feet, "Today is the first time I have thought of it, Charlotte. Wycherley will turn every deed back over to each of the indebted settlers should Adolphustown be victorious."

"Why would he make such a promise?" she hazarded to ask, "Why would a man so concerned with possessions be willing to risk it all over a boxing match?"

"He will still have lands here or in Marysburgh, depending on the winning side. Bets will undoubtedly be made from which he will find a way to gain," Sean explained. He paused as if he were unsure he should reveal the rest of what he was thinking, but finally he did.

"Boxing rules dictate that the fight must go on until one man is down and cannot get up. I do not wish to frighten you further, Charlotte, but some matches do end in a fighter's death. Wycherley sees me as a threat to his power here. Perhaps he wants me out of the way."

She gasped, clasping her hand to her chest, struggling to catch her breath. "Then you must not participate in this ridiculous spectacle!"

"If Adolphustown wins, he will also allow Caroline to go to Degan," Sean added.

"She is free to go to her child's father even without that awful man's permission!"

"Yet out of fear, she will not," Sean reminded her. He stood up and moved around the table to where she was standing. "It is a chance to free these people from Franklin Wycherley, Charlotte."

"But you would be the one to have to fight," Charlotte surmised.

Sean did not have to respond. They both knew the answer.

"And you think God will condone this fighting, even if it is for the people of Adolphustown?" she wondered.

"Few would believe this Charlotte, but as my wife, I hope you will. I did not throw a punch in those New York matches."

"Oh, Sean, how is that possible?" she asked, unbelieving.

"I dodged and dodged until my opponent tired so much that he could not continue," Sean insisted.

Charlotte looked skeptical. "I have never heard of such a thing," she told him, "A boxer who does not box?"

Sean nodded, "Any matches I've won since being ordained have not been without bloodshed, but I am proud to say that I have never struck a man unless he deserved it. I do believe God will forgive that much."

"So you can fight this man from Marysburgh without fighting him at all?" she asked.

"I was a younger man with more energy in those days, but I believe it is still possible, yes, Charlotte. And this will not help just the people, but the church's debt to Wycherley as well," he reminded her.

She seemed to give this some thought. Sean remained hopeful in the silence that followed. Surely she would see the merit in this idea.

"I cannot agree to this," she said suddenly, shaking her head and going back to her chair to sit down. "This is a test the Lord has laid out for you, Sean. You gave Him your word, and you must keep it!"

"I gave Father Weston my word!" he countered, "God will judge me his own way."

Charlotte took a deep breath. "There is something I must tell you, Sean, and it may explain to you my hesitation on this matter."

He saw the change in her expression and instantly he felt there was cause for concern. "What is it, darling?" he asked.

She exhaled deeply, "Perhaps it is as simple as asking yourself what one thing a woman could know before her husband," she replied.

Sean shook his head, "You know most things before I do," he admitted, "You often know what I am going to say long before I think of it, and you always know far more about Abigail than I could ever--" He stopped mid-sentence, and in spite of the seriousness of their previous conversation, the mood lightened considerably when he saw a grin spread across Charlotte's face. "Mrs. Brody, are you--?"

She nodded, laughing, and he bent down and wrapped his arms around her, picking her up and kissing her hard on the lips before swinging her around, nearly knocking the table over.

"Now you know why I do not want you to be part of this boxing folly," she told him as he set her down, "Your family needs you."

Sean felt as if his heart would burst with happiness. He nodded, tears filling his eyes. "We shall discuss it another time," he replied, "For now, it is time for rejoicing."

Another child, perhaps a boy this time, perhaps a second beautiful daughter. A playmate for Abigail. Unable to find words to express his joy, he simply leaned down and pulled Charlotte to him again.

"I love you, Sean," she whispered in his ear, "I love you so much."

CHAPTER TWELVE

The Van Horn cabin was already alive with people and music when the Brody's arrived. Window lamps offered a welcoming glow that lifted Charlotte's heart and spirit as they approached. She reached down and put a hand on her belly. It was still early in the pregnancy, but already she imagined she could feel a firmness that had not been there since she carried Abigail.

She glanced up at Sean and smiled, then felt Abigail let go of her free hand as she ran off to meet Emma, waiting patiently for her on the steps of the modest cabin.

Emma threw open the front door and they followed her inside to find settlers filling the main room, many gathered near the table that was set out with sandwiches, tea and sweets. Sean seemed more than happy to hand off the plate of tea cakes he'd been in charge of since they'd left the shanty. Charlotte went to the table and set them with the other refreshments, then turned and took in the festivities, a feeling of joyous celebration overwhelming her. It was not anything like the grandeur of her family's large society parties in Windsor, but it was a gathering of friends, nonetheless.

Walter Van Horn was in the corner, tapping his foot as he played a lively reel on his violin. Friends crowded nearby, clapping. Charlotte laughed, watching Abigail and Emma twirl about, their arms outstretched to one another as they danced in small circles together.

She glanced over at Sean, already deep in conversation with Willem and John Roberts. "You were discussing the boxing match with Marysburgh," she commented when he finally joined her.

"It is the talk of the town," Sean admitted, "They say that the fellow from Marysburgh is strong and well-built."

Charlotte glanced around the room. There were a handful of young men, though none were as large and hardy as Solomon Roberts. "Is there any chance that Solomon--"

Sean shook his head, already anticipating her question. "John says that his son is barely able to stand yet. The fight is in a month's time. He will not be ready."

Mary and Thomas Smythe brushed past on their way to the refreshment table. "Good evening, Mrs. Brody," Mary nodded.

"Good evening, Mary," Charlotte smiled, remembering the first day she had knocked on the Smythe's door. Mary's suspicions seemed to have dissipated since then. She and her family were in attendance at meeting house every Sunday, as were a number of settlers who had first given the preacher's wife nothing more than a cold stare. She glanced around the room, seeing Eliza and the widow Barker sitting together, chatting. Eliza waved and smiled.

The young Thurlow family were gathered in chairs near the fire, Nettie balancing two golden-haired toddlers on her lap, Abraham cradling their youngest in his arms. The child's head hung limply over his shoulder as she slept peacefully, no amount of music and loud chatter able to keep her from her slumber.

"This is a good place, Sean," Charlotte piped up out of the blue.

Sean swallowed the last bit of cookie he was working on and stared at Charlotte, narrowing his eyes in mock suspicion. "Either Willem has slipped something into your tea, or there has been a turn of events to change your mind about Adolphustown."

Since announcing her pregnancy, Charlotte seemed happier and more content, and for Sean, it almost felt as if things were as good as they could be. Now if only Judge Wycherley were somewhere else but here.

"Reverend Brody!"

They turned and saw Walter Van Horn's eldest son Joseph approaching.

"Joseph!" Sean extended a hand in greeting.

"Notice anything different about me?" Joseph asked.

Sean looked to Charlotte for a clue. "Did your mother cut your hair?" she asked curiously.

Joseph shook his head, his brown hair tied back with a ribbon. "No!"

Sean put a finger to his lips and, puzzled, looked Joseph up and down. "New buckles on your shoes?" he ventured cautiously.

"No!" Joseph replied, "Look at my shirt!"

"No frills!" Charlotte shouted victoriously.

"Correct!" Joseph exclaimed, "I was greatly moved during last Sunday's sermon, and I immediately had my mother remove the frills from all of my shirts!"

Sean nodded. "Your devotion is admirable, Mr. Van Horn, and

yet I do not remember outlawing frills."

"Reverend Culpepper asked it of us," Joseph explained, "But I did not listen. More than that, it was me who encouraged parties among our youth!"

Sean glanced at Charlotte and they shared a smile.

"No more frills!" Joseph exclaimed happily, "And no more parties for our young people! I want to learn from you, Reverend Brody. I want to be a Methodist preacher!"

"God bless you," Sean nodded.

"God help you," he heard Charlotte mutter under her breath.

"Pardon me, Mrs. Brody?" Joseph asked politely.

"Oh, nothing, Mr. Van Horn," Charlotte replied, "You will have a great teacher in Reverend Brody."

Joseph grinned and turned back to Sean. "I will see you on Sunday!" he beamed, then turned and left them.

"But we will not see his frills on Sunday," Charlotte giggled when he was out of earshot.

"His faith has been renewed, Charlotte," Sean said, directing her toward two empty chairs nearby, "We must encourage such enthusiasm."

Charlotte took Sean's hand in hers as they sat down. "You are right, husband. I do not mean to mock Joseph's devotion. In fact, I am proud of what you are accomplishing here against all odds."

"Every Sunday there are more at meeting house," Sean reminded her.

"That is because the people are finally beginning to trust you," Charlotte replied, "They look up to you. And that is why you must do it," she finished, leaning over to kiss him gently on the cheek.

It took Sean by surprise. "What is it that I must do?" he asked quizzically.

"You must take part in the boxing match," she replied, "I know it goes against what I first told you, but now I see that there is no one but you. These people are our neighbours, good neighbours, and they need you."

Sean slid his arm around her shoulder. "Are you absolutely certain, Charlotte?"

She nodded. "We have made so much progress here, Sean. More than I realized until now. God put us here for a reason. Perhaps he knew that you would be the only one who could help the people of the Fourth."

"And if it means the Bishop does not award us a better posting?" he ventured.

"Then that will be God's will," she replied. "There is only one condition in all of this, Sean."

"Go on then," he pressed, "What is it?"

"You must promise me that you will do this dodging that you mentioned."

Sean let out a chuckle. "This Marysburgh fellow may be large, but he is young and will not outmatch my experience. There will be no contest, Charlotte."

"Is this a serious conversation or may I join in?" Willem moved to the table, picked up a small sandwich, and gulped it down.

"Now that you mention it," Sean stood up and glanced happily at Charlotte, "There is something we had planned to announce this evening."

Charlotte nodded. "Now there are two announcements," she smiled.

"But one is more joyous, and that is what we will share with our friends tonight," he decided, "The other can wait until tomorrow."

"Well get on with it!" Willem encouraged, then turned to the room, "Everyone! Everyone! The Brody's have something to tell us!"

Walter abruptly ceased his fiddle playing as curious eyes turned in Sean and Charlotte's direction, watching expectantly.

"The Brody family is growing!" Sean announced happily, "Three will soon be four!"

A chorus of voices rose up in shouts of congratulatory approval, Eliza excitedly hurrying across the room to hug Charlotte, and the music started up again more joyous than ever.

*****

The days had been warm for two weeks, and rain only seemed to fall at night. It was just enough to keep the fields green, and the crops prospering. So too, did the church flourish. More settlers were attending services with every passing Sunday. Surprisingly,

Judge Wycherley had not yet taken any action in retaliation, the assumption being that Sean's decision to represent Adolphustown in the fight had placated the magistrate for now.

Sean looked over and smiled as Charlotte closed her eyes and raised her face to the sky, allowing the sun's rays to warm her skin. They were sitting on a log bench Sean had constructed just outside the shanty door. The tree stump that had once been their kitchen table sat nearby, always ready when Charlotte needed a place to set her laundry bucket. Abigail and Emma had gone to make mud pies on the clay shore, and all was well.

"You are glowing like the sun itself," Sean commented, smiling as he watched his beautiful wife put a hand to her belly, perhaps letting their child know that she was here waiting for him. He thought of Caroline Wycherley. No one had seen her for some time, and she would soon be due to give birth.

"Reverend!" Willem called from his yard, "Are you ready?"

Sean jumped to his feet and leaned down to kiss Charlotte on the cheek. "Will is helping me train today," he told her.

She furrowed her eyebrows in surprise. "I thought you said this opponent would be no match for your skills; that you will not have to throw a punch!"

"Even so, my darling," he grinned, "I cannot afford to be idle. He is still a young man – a blacksmith to boot! I am older and full of my wife's hearty cooking!"

"Many men would be happy to trade their solitary lives if only they could find a wife to cook for them!" she countered teasingly.

"I will not debate you on that point!" Sean laughed, "Oh, Charlotte, do you have vinegar in the kitchen?"

"Yes," she answered suspiciously, "What do you need with--"

Before she could finish asking the question, he had disappeared inside the shanty and returned with the vinegar.

"Thank you!" he called out, already on his way to meet Willem.

"Do not use it all!" she shouted as he left, then shook her head and sighed. She hoped she had done the right thing by giving Sean her blessing where this boxing match was concerned. However as she looked off into the distance to where the fight would be held, she heard the sound of hammers busy constructing the wooden stage that would serve as the ring, and it gave her little consolation.

*****

"Again!" Willem commanded, and Sean thrust his cloth-covered hand hard into the trunk of the oak tree. Bark flew in all directions, and Willem, already accustomed to it, quickly shielded his eyes from the assault. Sean exhaled loudly, leaned on the tree, and reached up to wipe the sweat from his brow. When he dropped his hand down again, Willem noticed the blood that was beginning to soak through the cloth. "I wouldn't let Charlotte see that if I were you," he suggested.

"The vinegar will help to toughen up the skin," Sean explained, unwrapping the cloth, "I soak my hands in it every day." He stuffed the fabric into his pocket, then turned and picked up an axe that was embedded into the top of a nearby tree stump.

"The afternoon's almost gone, Sean," Willem reminded him, "Perhaps you should save this for tomorrow."

"It will be an easy match to win if my opponent gives up as easily as you would like me to!" Sean replied, "You go home to your family, Will. I must cut down one more."

With that, he raised the axe and brought it down hard into the nearest birch tree.

"You'll soon have this piece of land cleared for me if you keep this up," Willem commented.

He patted Sean on the back, then picked up his water flask and wandered off back toward the settlement, the sharp chop of his friend's unyielding axe ringing through the forest well into late afternoon.

CHAPTER THIRTEEN

"Mr. Hawke!" Charlotte called out, catching up to Degan as he walked toward his canoe. Church had just let out, and she would not allow another week to pass without telling him the news she had so anxiously kept to herself.

Degan stopped and turned to her. "What is it, Mrs. Brody?"

Charlotte glanced around them to be sure there was no one else within earshot. Most of the settlers were moving away from the church toward their homes and buggies, and the handful of other Mohawks who had made the trip with Degan were busy preparing for the paddle home.

"Mr. Hawke," she repeated, lowering her voice so that only he could hear, "I have something of the greatest importance to tell you, but you must promise me that you will stay calm when all is revealed."

Deagan's relaxed facial expression did not change the way she had expected it would. Most people's eyes would fill with dread when about to hear uncertain news, or when being warned to remain calm no matter what. Charlotte paused and took a deep breath, then began, "Mr. Hawke, you should know that Miss Caroline Wycherley is...she is with child, and the baby is yours." She paused and watched his face, awaiting his reaction. When he gave no response she asked, "Did you hear what I said, Mr. Hawke?"

Degan's dark eyes softened, "I know about Caroline," he admitted.

Charlotte gasped. "How?" she wondered.

"I have been nearby, watching," he confessed, "I have seen her belly, but the Sheriff follows her closely when she leaves the house, and so I have not been able to speak to her for many weeks."

"She loves you," Charlotte told him.

He nodded. "I have a home waiting for her and our child. It's a good home, and I think she will like it, but she has not seen me in a long time. She might think I have abandoned her."

"I can help!" Charlotte offered impulsively, "I can bring her to you."

*****

Inside the meeting house, Sean collected his books and tucked them under his arm. Charlotte had left quickly, sending Abigail off with the Hollister clan, and he couldn't help but wonder what she might be up to.

Just as he was about to leave, a young man stepped inside and the two nearly collided. The man's black hair and tattered straw hat were familiar, and Sean instantly recognized him as one of the three men Wycherley had sent to the church some time before.

"I trust you have not brought your friends looking for any more trouble," Sean said immediately, "You remember what happened last time."

"They are not my friends," the man answered, removing his hat and timidly dropping his head. He raised his eyes to glance around the church, now empty of worshippers. "I have come for atonement," he mumbled.

Sean paused and regarded him closely, "Come and sit with me," he encouraged, and led the timid visitor to a pew.

When they were sitting comfortably, Sean put a hand on his shoulder. "What is your name, and what have you to say?" he asked.

"I am Andrew Owens," the man answered, pausing to take a deep breath, "I come from Marysburgh, and I helped beat a man to death. He was one of your own."

"Solomon Roberts," Sean nodded, "Is that who you mean?"

"The man who was to fight our fella from Marysburgh," Andrew nodded, "We were told to make sure he would never fight again."

"Who instructed you in this?" Sean asked.

Andrew paused.

"If you seek atonement," Sean explained, "Then you must confess everything."

"I'll be in an awful pile of trouble if I tell you who sent us," Andrew admitted anxiously.

"You have already told me too much to turn back," Sean explained, "Besides, oftentimes the most difficult thing and the right thing are the same. Considering the fact that you are here, Mr. Owen, I assume that you want to do the right thing."

Andrew nodded, "Alright then, though I'm sure you've already guessed. It was Judge Wycherley. He told us he would hurt our families if we didn't do it. It's just, I can't live with myself knowin' that fella almost died because of my own hand."

Sean exhaled deeply and patted Andrew reassuringly on the shoulder. "You've done the right thing today, Mr. Owen, and rest easy knowing this. The Roberts boy is on the mend, though it will be some time before he's well."

Andrew let out a huge breath of relief, "You can't know the weight you've just lifted from me, Reverend," he confessed.

"In the meantime," Sean continued, "His father is missing his help on the farm. Hurting one person hurts many, Andrew."

"I know that now, Reverend," Andrew replied, "I'm just so glad it wasn't worse. The way he looked when we ran from him...I was certain we had--" The young man drooped forward, his body limp with relief, and tears streamed from his eyes, "Thank God," he choked, "Thank God!"

"Yes," Sean raised up his voice and looked to the rafters, "Let us thank God for bringing the truth into the light!" He turned back to Andrew, "And now, son, there is one thing more that you must do in order to receive complete absolution."

*****

"How long will you be gone?" Sean asked, watching Charlotte put the last few things into the picnic basket on the table.

"Only a short while," Charlotte answered absently, scrunching up her face in concentration as she scanned the cupboards to be sure she hadn't forgotten anything.

"I have still to finish Sunday's sermon," Sean reminded her, "And I must train--"

"And you must replace the vinegar again," Charlotte interrupted, "There's none to be found every time I want to make a vinegar pie."

"Abigail and I will go to Mr. Hanley's today to get some," he assured her. "Charlotte, do you honestly think that Caroline Wycherley will feel up to a picnic in the woods?" he wondered, "I can't imagine it would be good for her to be sitting on the damp ground."

"I will find a comfortable spot," Charlotte replied, covering the basket with a cloth, "Abigail and Emma have gone to pick berries with Eliza, but they should be back soon."

She brushed past Sean and leaned up to kiss him quickly on the lips.

"Be careful!" he warned her, "Cain won't be far behind!"

"I'll see about that," Charlotte called back over her shoulder on her way out. A few minutes later, she was negotiating with Lucy at the Wycherley's front door.

"The Judge says Miss Caroline can't have no company," the young servant shook her head, "She's gettin' close to her time."

"Well, I have brought some lunch to help her keep up her strength," Charlotte smiled, "And a little fresh air will do her good."

In spite of Lucy nearly blocking the doorway, Charlotte stepped in and moved around her, "Caroline?" she called out, glancing up the stairs.

"What's this?" Sheriff Cain appeared at the end of the hall and slowly approached. It was common knowledge that he lived in a cabin on the Wycherley property, but Charlotte wondered how much time he actually spent in their house to keep an eye on Caroline.

"Oh," she exclaimed, feigning surprise, "I thought you would be at the tavern."

"Why would I be at the tavern?" Cain asked, puzzled.

"Because there's trouble there," Charlotte lied, "When I walked past, there were two men on the front steps quarrelling, and a crowd was gathering around them."

Cain's eyes narrowed. "Get my hat," he said sideways to Lucy, not unlocking his stare on Charlotte, and the nervous servant went scurrying over to the peg board.

"Miss Wycherley's sleeping, Mrs. Brody," he cautioned, "You'd best come back later."

Lucy jumped in quickly to help, "Judge Wycherley's indeed sleepin' but I don't think that Miss Caroline is--"

"Get back to the kitchen and tend to your duties!" Cain snapped, cutting her off.

"Yes, sir," Lucy nodded obediently, "Good day, Mrs. Brody."

Charlotte's polite smile hid the sinking feeling that the

retreating Lucy might have been a great help to her. "I'll just leave this here in case Caroline would like it when she wakes," she told Cain, setting the lightly-packed picnic basket on the floor at her feet, "Good day."

Cain followed her out of the house, quickly overtaking her and hurrying ahead on his way to the tavern. Charlotte slowed her steps, and when he was safely out of sight she turned quickly back to the house, quietly opened the door, grabbed the picnic basket, and crept up the stairs.

Charlotte carefully navigated the hallway, peering into rooms and praying she would not bump into Judge Wycherley. Her fears were relieved when she heard thunderous snoring, and pushing open a door that was slightly ajar, she saw him lying on his bed fully-clothed, his hands resting on his huge belly.

Moving quietly away from the room, she finally discovered Caroline sitting in a rocking chair near the half-open window in her bed chamber. She was staring out at the grove of maple trees that filled the back yard, her large round belly looking nearly ready to burst. She turned when she heard Charlotte enter the room.

"Mrs. Brody!" she exclaimed.

"Shhh!" Charlotte warned, putting a finger to her lips, "Do not wake the judge. No one knows I am here, and we must leave quickly."

"Leave?" Caroline asked, bewildered.

"You told me that you would be with Degan Hawke if you could. Do you still feel that way?"

"Yes!" Caroline exclaimed, "Yes, Mrs. Brody! I would give anything!"

"Then come with me now," Charlotte told her, helping Caroline slowly up from her chair, "Degan will meet us at the shore. And please call me Charlotte."

A look of dreaded realization suddenly crossed Caroline's face, and she drew back a little, "My father will have Degan killed! He will have us both killed!"

Charlotte grabbed Caroline's hands and squeezed them gently to calm her. "The Mohawks will not let him hurt you. Degan has already told them you are to be his wife."

"His wife?" Caroline repeated, as if in a trance, "We are to be married?"

124

"They are readying things now at the Mohawk settlement," Charlotte smiled, "You and Degan will be married by the time your child is born."

Caroline smiled and nodded, "Forgive me Mrs. Brody – Charlotte, but this is all happening so quickly!" she admitted.

"Let us pack some things in this picnic basket," Charlotte instructed, "Quickly now, there is no time to waste!"

They left the house quietly, and when they were safely out of view, Charlotte carefully took Caroline's arm and led her down toward the clay shore. They travelled along the water's edge and away from the settlement for several minutes until a canoe appeared, moving toward them.

Caroline squinted in the sunlight. "Degan!" she cried out happily.

Charlotte wrapped a comforting arm around Caroline's waist to calm her. "Are you ready to go with him now?" she asked, "For after this, there will be no turning back."

Caroline nodded, gazing longingly toward Degan as he paddled closer. Tears filled her eyes when he finally pulled the canoe up onto the shore and began to walk toward them.

"Degan!" she called out again, her voice half excitement, half sobbing.

Charlotte stepped back and swallowed hard, a lump in her throat and tears in her eyes as she watched them fall into one another's arms.

*****

"How was your picnic?" Sean asked. Abigail was nestled in his lap, a favourite dolly in her arms as Charlotte prepared their supper. She shrugged and did not turn around to face him.

"Charlotte?" he repeated.

"You know how picnics are, Sean," she answered impatiently, "Abigail, you should wash those dirty hands before supper."

Abigail jumped from her comfortable spot, dropped the doll into her father's lap, and went to the wash stand. Just tall enough to reach up to it, she perched up on her toes and dipped her hands into the water basin.

"Degan and I are going fishing later this week," Sean

commented absently.

"Fishing?" Charlotte exclaimed, swinging around to face him.

"Yes," Sean laughed softly, "As we have done at least twice in the past few weeks." He paused. "Is there something the matter, Charlotte?"

"Of course not," she replied, turning back to the counter, "It is only that sometimes unexpected events can change one's plans. Perhaps you should not count on fishing with Mr. Hawke."

"I cannot imagine that there have been any unexpected events in Degan's life," Sean scrunched up his face the way he did when he was quite perplexed, "Besides that, he's across the bay, Charlotte. Shall I send up smoke signals to ask him if he's still able to go fishing?"

There was a loud knock at the door and Charlotte jumped, startled. She turned and watched as Sean got up from his chair, but she went back to her duties just as quickly when she saw that it was Sheriff Cain who had come calling. He glanced past Sean into the shanty.

"What business have you here, Mr. Cain?" Sean asked suspiciously, doing his best to fill the doorway so that the sheriff would not be able to squeeze in.

"Lookin' for Caroline Wycherley," Cain nodded, "She here?"

"Not unless she's simmering in a cooking pot," Sean joked, "Why would Miss Wycherley be here?"

"Maybe your wife can answer that question," Cain suggested, nodding in Charlotte's direction.

Sean turned and glanced at Charlotte.

"I joined Caroline Wycherley for a picnic today," she nodded, wiping her hands on a kitchen cloth as she turned and walked slowly toward them, "And I watched her leave for home afterward. That's the last I've seen of her."

"You sent me on a wild goose chase to the tavern to put me off 'yer trail," Cain raised his voice accusingly.

"There was no scuffle when you arrived?" Charlotte exclaimed in mock surprise.

"Now look here--" he attempted to step past Sean, but he might as well have tried to walk through a wall.

"My wife has told you that Miss Wycherley returned home after their picnic," Sean insisted, wrapping a firm hand around

Cain's arm, "Now instead of looking for blame where there is none, I suggest you devote your ambition to finding the missing young lady."

Cain let out a frustrated breath and pulled his arm free, "There'll be trouble if you've had anything to do with this," he warned, tossing a backward glance at Charlotte as he walked away.

Sean closed the door and faced his wife. "What happened today?" he asked, keeping his voice low.

"Caroline and I had a picnic and we each returned home, just as I told Sheriff Cain," she replied innocently, then turned back to the kitchen.

"And you're not concerned that Miss Wycherley is unaccounted for?" Sean wondered.

Charlotte paused, dropped the kitchen cloth on the counter, and turned to him. "She went home, Sean. To the place where she belongs, where she and her child will be happy."

Sean thought for minute, then nodded in realization. "You took her to Degan."

"She wanted to go," Charlotte shrugged, "She is in love with him. She is having his child."

"Did you give any thought to how Wycherley might react when he finds out?" Sean wondered.

"No, frankly, I gave no thought to that horrid man at all," Charlotte answered curtly, "Though Degan did, and he assured me that his people will be ready should Wycherley threaten anyone in their settlement."

"You may have put people in danger, Charlotte," Sean scolded.

"We have to stand up for what is right, Sean Brody," she reminded him, "Even if it frightens us. I learned that from you."

He let out an exasperated sigh. "And to think I sometimes fear that no one is paying attention to my sermons."

"Well I pay attention every time," she nodded, "And your words do stay with me, Mr. Brody, whether you like them tossed back at you or not."

He chuckled, going to her, "As long as that's all you're throwing at me this time," he grinned.

Charlotte sighed and wrapped her arms around him, "Imagine what it would have been like had someone kept us apart, Sean."

"Well, you've got to admit your parents did give it a fairly decent try," he joked, kissing the top of her head, and she laughed quietly.

"I do understand why you did it, Charlotte," he continued, "But taking that young woman away from Franklin Wycherley could drum up all manner of troubles for us, just when things seemed to be starting to settle down here in the Fourth."

*****

A few days after Caroline's departure, a notice tacked to the board outside the tavern read, *"Notice: All are warned against trusting my daughter, Caroline Wycherley, on my account, as I will not pay any debts contracted by her after this date, she having left my home and board without my consent." - Franklin J. Wycherley, Adolphustown*

"It seems that money is of greater importance to him than even his family," Sean observed, relaying the information to Charlotte.

"Riches are the devil's temptation," she reminded him, "And if anyone in Adolphustown is in league with the devil, it is Judge Wycherley."

*****

It was a perfect night for fishing. Sean found the Bay of Quinte to be the most peaceful place his travels had ever taken him. Any worries he may have had about the upcoming boxing match were washed away as he sat by the light of the pitch pine torch in the canoe with Degan.

"Do you think you can beat him?" Degan asked from his seat in the bow, a lengthy fish spear in his right hand. His long dark hair was pulled into one long braid down his back.

"I haven't seen him," Sean admitted, "Will Hollister tells me he is younger than me by ten years, but no match for my experience."

"You must respect your enemy," Degan suggested, "Never go into battle assuming that you will win."

"I never have," Sean confirmed, "I am training with Will every day."

"Good," Degan nodded, his eyes on the water, and suddenly he sprang up and thrust his spear effortlessly beneath the surface. When he pulled it back up, a large bass thrashed on the tip, and he quickly deposited it into the large bucket of water brought along for that purpose. "At the same time," Degan continued, his eyes scanning the water again, "There is nothing wrong with letting your enemy think that you are less than him. Then surprise him with the truth when he least expects it."

Degan drew back suddenly as Sean's spear flew past him, and this time a large pickerel was impaled.

"I do not take my enemy for granted," Sean nodded, pulling the spear and its scaly passenger back into the boat, "And yes, hopefully my enemy will take me for granted," he smiled.

Degan grinned.

"How is Caroline?" Sean asked, dropping the fish into the bucket.

Degan's face went somber. "She is worried about having the baby at the village," he confessed, "Our ways are different in such things."

"You will need to be wary of Wycherley," Sean warned.

Degan shook his head. "He has already sent word to Caroline that she is no longer welcome in his home, and though she despises him, she has not been easily consoled since. She considered him family. Now she feels alone, though I am with her."

Sean nodded. "It will not be easy for her there," he suggested. "Charlotte thought you might not come tonight so that you could stay with her."

"The women will keep close watch," Degan confirmed, "They will send a signal if anything happens." He suddenly shot up to his feet and thrust his spear into the water again. "In the meantime," he continued, plopping the fish into the bucket, "Unborn babies have all the food they need, but the rest of us still need to eat."

CHAPTER FOURTEEN

It was still morning, but already the sun blazed hot upon the newly-constructed boxing stage. Today it served a nefarious purpose, but Sean already had plans as to how it would be used in the future, there being a need for such a platform at the camp meeting that he and Ezra Beckett were planning for the fall. He felt a twinge of nervousness as he approached the throng of spectators gathered for the match. It was reminiscent of a carnival atmosphere, people having travelled to the Fourth from townships far afield, and he understood why when he glanced over and noticed a hastily-erected betting post set a good distance away from the stage. He had figured there would be more at stake for Wycherley than land claims. The magistrate would profit from this match in every way he could.

Sean jumped up onto the stage, and Willem, acting as his Second, followed close behind. A hearty roar went up from the eager crowd when they appeared, and Sean instinctively raised his hands in the air to show his appreciation.

"Where's the Marysburgh fellow?" he wondered aloud, glancing around.

The moment he'd asked the question, the crowd fell silent and parted to make way for his opponent.

"I'm betting he's not from Marysburgh," Willem said soberly as both of them watched a huge castle of a man step up onto the stage, his chest heaving in anticipation of the battle. The sweat on his bald head dripped down onto his heavily scarred face, his angry eyes fixed on Sean.

The boxer grinned at Sean and nodded, shouting across the stage, "I'm back to finish the job, Brody!"

Another huge roar went up from the crowd, and a flurry of people went running toward the betting post.

"Dear Lord, Sean...do you know him?" Willem asked.

"Ruthless Rufus Ryan," Sean nodded, sizing up his opponent, "The only man I've never been able to defeat." He took a deep breath, "He almost killed me in Boston."

"You can't fight him!" Willem immediately responded, "We must put a stop to this now!"

Sean reached out and grabbed Will's arm before he could move away toward the umpire. "I have to fight him," he insisted, "It's the only way to put a stop to Wycherley once and for all."

With that, he pulled at the drawstring that tightened his breeches and started confidently toward the chalk line that was drawn across the centre of the stage.

*****

Charlotte focused on her needlework as a flurry of excited feet passed in front of her. Eliza sat in the chair beside her, looking off in the direction of the temporary boxing ring that had been built in the clearing well away from the church and cabins.

The Hollister children sat on the grass nearby, Phoebe entertaining Zedekiah. Emma and Abigail sat not far away, dollies sitting idle in their laps as they peered along the path toward the main event.

"Mama, please!" Abigail begged, "What if Papa needs help?"

"Your father can take care of himself," Charlotte nodded, though she could not resist glancing off in the distance, the voices growing louder as the crowd grew in rapidly increasing numbers.

"Perhaps we could just watch for a few minutes!" Emma suggested, rising up on her knees to look at her mother.

Eliza frowned. "Emma!"

Without another word Emma picked up her doll and pretended to return to play.

In the distance, a roar of approval could be heard from the crowd.

"I couldn't have stopped him even if I had tried," Charlotte murmured absently to no one in particular, "Sean Brody goes his own way. But that doesn't mean I always have to follow."

Hurried footsteps approached, and eighteen year-old Bram Hollister appeared. "You should see the Marysburgh fella!" he shouted excitedly, "He's even bigger than Reverend Brody!"

Charlotte stood up and set her needlepoint on the chair, glancing at Eliza. "Oh no," she frowned.

"Someone needs to stay with the children," Eliza reminded her friend, "You go. I'll watch them."

Arriving at scene, Charlotte struggled to push through the

crowd to get a better look. Peering up toward the stage she could see Sean, wearing only his breeches. His face and chest glistened with sweat, and as far as she could tell, the fight hadn't even begun yet.

"Sean!" she called out, the crowd opening up to let her through as she made her way to the side of the stage. She gasped when she turned to look at his opponent.

Sean approached and whispered, "You should not be here!"

"Sean, you cannot!" she protested, "He is huge!" She put a hand to her stomach, her eyes filling with tears. "I have changed my mind, Sean, I do not want you to be hurt. Please!"

Sean's eyes filled with regret, but it did not change his mind. "I will be fine. I have no choice, Charlotte," he insisted.

"There is always a choice," she reminded him, "There has to be a better way."

Sean nodded. "This is the only way. I have made a promise to the people of Adolphustown, and I must show them that they can depend on my word."

"Reverend Brody!"

Charlotte swung around at the sound of Wycherley's voice.

"What is the delay?" Wycherley rose from the chair he had been sitting on near the stage and slowly approached. "Oh, Mrs. Brody!" he smiled, "You've come to see your husband champion the people of Adolphustown."

"This must end now!" Charlotte demanded, glancing again at the Marysburgh man who stared down at her, his teeth bared as if he were an animal preparing for the kill.

Wycherley let out a raspy laugh. "I am afraid your husband is committed to this match," he informed her, "Besides, it is all in good fun. This is a day for the community to come together in fellowship and be entertained."

"This is barbarism!" she shouted, "That man is no Marysburgh blacksmith! He is obviously is a trained fighter, and no one yearns to be witness to such a spectacle."

"Get on with it!" someone shouted.

"Fight him, Reverend!" another voice yelled, "It won't be any worse than the pounding Solomon Roberts took!"

More voices rose up in agreement.

Wycherley smiled smugly, "The eager crowd belies your

opinion, Mrs. Brody. Now please be on your way. You are holding things up."

He waved his cane in the air as if to move things along, then turned and made his way back to his chair.

"He is right, darling," Sean nodded, leaning down to be closer to her, "You must go. This will be over soon enough, and then I promise you will never have to worry about me fighting again."

"I am fearful, Sean," Charlotte argued, wiping away a tear, "What shall I do?"

"You must go and let me handle this now, Charlotte," he advised her, "Go home and be with Abigail," he told her softly, moving forward to kiss her on the forehead, "I will be there soon."

He watched as she looked up toward the giant at the other side of the stage and shouted, "He is a father with a duty to his family and his community, and if you dare hurt him, I swear it's me you will answer to!"

The man grinned at her bravado, and the crowd responded with laughter and applause. She had said her piece, but Charlotte's heart was pounding with fear for her husband as she turned and walked away. Tears dripped down her cheeks, and her mind was reeling with worry as she neared the shanty. Preoccupied with her thoughts, it was doubly unnerving when a hand reached out and grabbed her arm. Her head snapped around as she instinctively pulled away from the man's grip, suddenly noticing that it was a friend at her side.

"Degan!" she exclaimed with relief, "You frightened me! Whatever are you doing here?"

"You must help!" he insisted, "Caroline felt she was close to her time and wanted to be with you when the baby comes. We brought the canoe across and I carried her as far as I could along the shore. She is in so much pain, Mrs. Brody!"

A new kind of fear gripped Charlotte. She glanced back toward the fight, wanting to be there should Sean need her, but knowing he did not want her there. Common sense took over, and she nodded to Degan. "Take me to her," she instructed, "We must bring her to the settlement."

As they hurried toward the path, Charlotte saw a dark-skinned man walking up from the bay with a fresh catch of fish still flailing about in the bucket. She'd never met him, but she knew who he was.

"Mr. Braswell?"

The man hesitated and glanced suspiciously at Charlotte and Degan.

"I know your wife, Betsey," Charlotte explained quickly, "We need your help!"

A scream rang out from the forest, and Calvin Braswell hastily set down his bucket and fish spear to unquestioningly follow them along the path.

"Degan!" Caroline called out.

Finally arriving at her side, Charlotte quickly surveyed the situation and felt a sense of foreboding. Degan dropped down beside them and took Caroline's hand. "I am here, my love," he told her softly.

Caroline grabbed on to his arm, wincing in pain, and he looked helplessly at Charlotte. "Please help her!" he pleaded.

"Lift her carefully," Charlotte instructed. She knew that Eliza and the children were still outside the Hollister cabin, but when she announced that this was their destination, Caroline panicked.

"Please hurry!" she shouted, "Please!"

"We are nearly there, Caroline, just hold on!" Charlotte urged. As they neared the Hollister's, Eliza saw what was transpiring and ran to meet them.

"Here!" Charlotte directed them to lay Caroline on the large blanket that the children had been sitting on.

"Bring Betsey!" Charlotte told Calvin, and he turned and sprinted away in the direction of his cabin.

Eliza sent the children inside the cabin, then dropped down onto the blanket and sat cross-legged, resting Caroline's head in her lap.

It seemed an eternity, but when Calvin finally arrived back on the scene with Betsey, Charlotte moved out of the way to let the midwife take charge.

'This baby needs to be born," Betsey muttered, pushing Caroline's skirts up around her waist, "God bless this mother and baby."

Eliza wiped the sweat from Caroline's face with a towel.

"Get that away from me!" Caroline shouted, grabbing the cloth and throwing it away.

"My goodness!" Eliza exclaimed in surprise.

"I want rum!" Caroline yelled.

Charlotte glanced at Betsey, on her knees at Caroline's feet. "It wouldn't hurt her none," she shrugged.

Charlotte nodded at Eliza, then tightened her grip as Caroline grabbed on to her hand and held on through another long push.

"Girls!" Eliza called toward the cabin. Abigail and Emma appeared in the doorway, their eyes wide with wonder as they stared down at Caroline.

"Emma!" Eliza shouted, "Go to the tavern and bring the fancy bottle your father keeps in his drawer!"

"But Papa says I am never to take--"

"Quickly!" Eliza demanded, "He will understand!"

Caroline was screaming out in pain when they returned with the rum.

"Finally there's a good use for this," Eliza commented as she gently lifted Caroline's head and held the bottle to her mouth so that she could drink.

Nearby, Degan paced back and forth, glancing toward the women each time Caroline let out another anguished cry. Finally he approached them. "She should be on her feet!" he told them, "It will help the baby to come easier. I have heard this from the Mohawk women."

Charlotte glanced at Eliza with questioning eyes.

"Willem will tell you it was me who wore the path to the church walking back and forth as each of mine came," Eliza shrugged, "But that doesn't mean it's the same for everyone."

"Betsey?" Charlotte ventured.

"If she feels she can do it, I can't see the harm in it," she nodded.

"I want to try!" Caroline nodded breathlessly, "Please, help me up!"

Degan leaned down and helped the women slowly ease Caroline up, first on to her knees, then onto her feet.

"I can't, I can't..." Caroline quickly changed her mind and they lowered her back down again, but she only made it to her knees before grimacing as another wave of pain washed over her. Betsey placed a firm hand on Caroline's stomach, reached down to lift her skirts up out of the way again and said, "Your baby is coming now.

It will not be much longer."

*****

Sean felt the crush of the crowd around the stage as the heat of the day bore down, even as his opponent's steely gaze cut into him. He reached up with his hardened hands and did his best to wipe the sweat from his eyes, but still he felt it running down his face, along his neck and back, and onto his bare chest.

He took himself back to his first fight with Rufus Ryan, heard the crowd shouting, felt himself wavering, stumbling, until the final bare-knuckle knockout punch was delivered. The room went black. It was as close to death as he'd ever been.

"Let's get to the scratch, Sean," Will encouraged, slapping him on his sweaty back, and Sean nodded, stepping forward into the chalk square in the center of the stage.

Sheriff Cain, acting as Ryan's Second, escorted his man to the other side of the scratch, and the two giants stood facing each other, legs spread in a confident stance, each eyeing the other as a wolf might regard its prey.

The skinny postmaster from Bath, an avid boxing fan, had agreed to Umpire the match, and he eagerly stepped up onto the stage to make the starting announcement. "Once the match begins," he called out, scanning the crowd in all directions as he spoke, "Fighting will continue until a man is down. He will be allowed thirty seconds to rest before returning to the scratch, and if he cannot return to the scratch on his own steam in those thirty seconds, the fight will be over, and his opponent will be declared the winner. Seconds, please leave the stage."

"Win this, Sean!" Will slapped his friend on the cheek as if to wake him up.

Sean nodded, his eyes still on Ryan, and he jumped back and forth from one foot to the other, his heart pounding in his chest.

"Begin!"

The command set something on fire in Sean. A hundred fights came flooding back. Instinctively he wanted to move forward and throw as many punches as he could land, but he had made a promise. He would avoid shedding another man's blood if he could, even if it was Ruthless Rufus Ryan, the man who'd nearly killed him.

Ryan took advantage of Sean's hesitation, moving forward and punching quickly left, then right. Sean ducked and dodged, snapping out of the way through every attempt Ryan made to make contact with his opponent's head. This game of cat and mouse continued for what may have seemed like an eternity for the unsatisfied crowd, shouting, "Hit him!" "Punch him!" Some pounded their fists on the stage, as if that might send a signal to Sean Brody to get in the game, shed some blood, give people what they came for. But it had been four rounds, and Sean was tiring.

Ryan smirked, by now perhaps realizing that the preacher had made a silent vow to resist fighting. He came forward in a fury, landing one blow after another to the preacher's stomach, another to the side of his head, then a heavy kick to his midsection.

Sean's knees went out from under him and he dropped, exhausted, to the stage. He felt cold water pouring over his head and heard Will in his ear. "Get up, Sean!" he demanded, "You must get up and fight!"

Determined not to disappoint the people of Adolphustown, Sean planted his hands on the stage and pushed himself up, got back on his feet, and somehow managed to stagger back to the scratch just as he heard the Postmaster's voice rise up above the crowd to announce, "Round Five!"

Again, Ryan came at him, barely breathing heavy, his punches fast and controlled. Sean tasted blood in his mouth. He was beginning to realize he could not win this match without fighting.

"Hit him or he'll kill you for good this time, Sean!" he heard Will shout.

He didn't know if his blurry vision was owing to the punches or the film of sweat that covered his face, but he could see clearly enough to know that Ryan coming at him again.

"God forgive me," Sean whispered under his breath, and as Ryan came near, he launched a blow directly at the unsuspecting man's head.

A cheer went up from the crowd louder than any Sean had ever heard. Ryan floundered for a moment, shaking off the surprise blow, and Sean hit him again. Ryan stumbled backward, and Sean knew he almost had him.

"One more good punch, Sean!" he could hear Daniel shouting

all the way from Vermont, "One more good punch and we'll be riding in a golden carriage!"

Sean danced forward, his energy renewed, and approached Ryan to land the final blow, but he had to pull back when Rufus dropped to his knees.

Backing up to his side of the scratch, Sean waited to see what would happen, praying Ryan wouldn't make it back to the square in time. Victory was imminent.

"Wait!" Cain yelled out, "Brody has something in his hands!"

"What?" Sean shouted, confused.

Hoots went up throughout the crowd as Will jumped up onto the stage and stepped forward to protest. "This is not right!" he shouted, "Ryan is down and it will soon be thirty seconds! Look at him!"

Ryan was still on his knees, his eyes barely open. Cain rushed forward and poured a bucket of water on him, slapping his face in encouragement.

The postmaster entered the stage, shaking his head. "We must investigate this claim!" he announced, stepping over to Sean. "Open your hands!" he demanded.

Sean's hands, clamped tightly shut for so many rounds, felt like rusted hinges covered in sweat as he slowly opened them, shaking, revealing nothing.

The postmaster nodded and turned back to the crowd, "There is nothing in his hands, the fight will continue. Seconds off the stage, please!"

"This fight was over!" Will protested, following the postmaster off to the side of the stage, "This was only a ruse to allow Ryan time to regain his strength!"

"Seconds off the stage!" the Umpire shouted again.

There were scattered jeers from the crowd, no doubt from those who had put their money on Sean to win, but this soon turned to cheers of excitement when Ruthless Rufus once again stood facing The Preacher.

Sean collected himself, staring hard at Rufus. Brute instinct flooded over him. His family needed him. The people of the Fourth needed him. He would not allow anyone to take his life from him without a fight. He knew what needed to be done.

Ryan looked weakened, but he wouldn't give up. Sean knew

that about him already. There was still a fight ahead, and the longer the men stood facing each other, shoulders heaving, sweat dripping, the more the fervor of the crowd grew.

"Kill him!" Wycherley screamed, jumping to his feet.

Sean froze and looked at the portly magistrate. Time stopped as the real reason behind this match came home to him. Wycherley had it planned from the start. He'd looked into Sean's past, found the one man who could match him, and brought him to Adolphustown to kill the new preacher. It wasn't uncommon for a man to die on the boxing stage. And so it would be nice and legal, just the way Wycherley managed to do everything.

"Sean!" Will's voice boomed into his thoughts and Sean came around just in time to see huge, bloody bare knuckles in front of his face. He darted to the right, caught Ryan hard in the stomach with his left fist as he moved, and watched as Rufus went spiraling backward. It happened in a second, but Sean somehow saw it in slow time as the gigantic boxer lost his balance in the corner, the back of his head connecting with the top of the corner post. A sharp "crack" could be heard as he went down, immediately followed by the deathly hush that fell over the amazed crowd.

The Umpire jumped excitedly onto the stage and rushed toward the corner, counting out loud, "5…6…7…8…"

Sean stood watching, breathing heavy, praying to God that Rufus was not dead, and at the same time hoping that he would not get up.

"13…14…15…"

"Hold on, Sean!" he heard Will yell, "You've got him! Hold on!"

"Get up!" Wycherley screamed from the side of the stage, "Get up you useless brute!"

Cain moved as close as he could get to Ryan's position, but the rules wouldn't let him interfere unless it was to declare his fighter beaten. Sean knew better than to hope for such a miracle.

"20…21…22…"

Ryan began to move his head from side to side, mumbling. Sean clenched his fists together anxiously. He remembered having the same feeling on days his father had arrived home after working long hours on a farm that would never be his, falling behind on rent owed to a wealthy absentee landlord, and looking to take out his frustrations on a young son who would offer no challenge. Until he grew bigger.

"29...30!"

The silent crowd suddenly found the voice to roar its approval, and Will jumped onto the stage, grabbing Sean around the waist and trying to lift him up into the air. Sean shook his head and looked over to the corner. Rufus was moving slowly, not dead, but quite injured.

"You did it, Sean!" Will yelled, "You did it!"

Sean nodded, finally realizing it wasn't a dream. He had beaten Ruthless Rufus Ryan. The people of Adolphustown were free of Franklin Wycherley's tyranny. But just to be sure of it, Sean had one more order of business to attend to.

CHAPTER FIFTEEN

Sean peered ahead through red, swollen eyes and saw the crowd waiting near the tavern steps as he walked back toward the shanty. Will was at his side, eager to meet the group of excited men who descended upon them with congratulatory cheers. Charlotte pushed through the crowd toward them.

"Are you alright, Sean?" she worried, her eyes filling with tears as she reached a hand up toward his bloodied face.

He nodded and smiled. "It looks far worse than it feels," he assured her.

Charlotte smiled with relief. "Caroline and Degan have a son," she said proudly, "They named him Sean. Sean Hawke."

Sean grinned and grabbed her around the waist, lifting her up into the air as she laughed. When he set her down, Abigail was at his side, pulling at his shirt.

"We won Papa, didn't we?" she cried out happily.

"We won, Little Abigail, yes we did!" Sean laughed, reaching down to tap her on the nose, but noting that her eyes turned grave when she saw his bloodied face. "It is alright, Little Abigail," he soothed, squatting down to wrap an arm gently around her, "Do not be frightened. It will all wash away in time."

Her concern turned to excitement. "Papa!" she exclaimed, "If you won the fight, what does the other man's face look like?"

There were scattered laughs, but Charlotte quickly cleared her throat to quiet them and gazed sternly at Sean, "I am sure the other man will be just fine, won't he, Reverend Brody?"

Sean glanced up at her, "Oh, yes, yes!" he nodded, rising to his feet and giving Abigail's hand a squeeze, "He is in a wagon on his way home, and he will be right as royalty soon enough!"

"Reverend Brody won far more than a boxing match today!" someone shouted, and there were more cheers.

"Which reminds me," Sean raised his voice so all could hear, "Judge Wycherley was to have handed over the deeds and signed off on all debts on the stage at the end of the match, but he made a quick departure." Jeers of disappointment followed. "I am on my way to see him now," Sean added, "And I encourage all of you to come along so that we, as a town, can be sure that all that is owed will be returned."

The crowd chatted agreeably between themselves, but Charlotte was still worried for her husband's safety. "Sheriff Cain will have his pistol at the ready, Sean, especially if he sees a mob approaching!"

"This mob will serve as witness to anything that happens between me and Wycherley," he reassured her, "And we have two more to collect along the way who will be the greatest help of all. Do not worry, darling," and he kissed her on the forehead.

"Let us walk together," Sean called out, urging the group forward.

*****

"You surprise me, Reverend Brody," Wycherley mused as Sean stepped into his study, "Who would have thought that a man of God could be capable of such brutality?"

"Expansion is the true mark of a man, Judge Wycherley," Sean reminded him, as Will stepped into the room behind him.

Voices could be heard rising up from outside the study window, and Cain rushed in to draw back the curtain. "He's brought the whole town with him!" he shouted.

Wycherley waved him off, "Get out," he ordered, and Cain hesitantly exited, leering hatefully at Sean as he went.

Wycherley opened a drawer, producing a stack of loose documents, "Most of these properties are hardly worth the parchment they're printed on," he shrugged, "It will take years to clear much of the land in the Fourth."

"We have the people and the determination to do it," Willem piped up.

"Have you heard that Caroline had a son?" Sean asked.

"That woman has made her own bed," Wycherley replied, "Literally. Now she must lie in it. I care not what she does." He picked up a quill pen and dipped it in the inkwell on his desk, beginning to sign over the documents.

"You have lost so much more than a boxing match," Sean suggested, watching him write.

Wycherley straightened up a little in response. "The betting post returns tell a different story, Reverend."

"I'm not talking about money, Judge Wycherley, and I fear that you have made your own bed as well."

Sean thought he saw a hint of regret in Wycherley's eyes, but the judge quickly turned back to the task at hand. "If you're speaking of Caroline, she was never really my daughter to begin with. Besides, she is too much like her wayward mother was at that age. My marrying her would not have helped her one bit."

"I agree," Sean replied, "She is far better off with Mr. Hawke."

Wycherley sniffed haughtily and finished what he was writing, pushing the papers to the edge of the desk as Willem moved forward to inspect them.

"Is everything in order, Will?" Sean asked.

"I will take them outside to the others," Willem answered, moving toward the study door and leaving it open as he left the room.

"We have business left to discuss," Sean informed Wycherley, "That wasn't a fair fight."

Wycherley chuckled. "A public boxing match officiated by an Umpire and following Broughton's Rules is fair game, Reverend Brody. No one should know that better than you."

"That's not the fight I'm speaking of," Sean shook his head, "Three armed men ambushing one who is unarmed. Is that fair game as well, Judge Wycherley?"

"I think you sustained a few too many hits to the head today, Brody," Wycherley replied, "For I have no idea what you are talking about."

"Perhaps this gentleman can help rekindle your memory," Sean offered, and looking over his shoulder he called out, "Come in, please."

Sean watched Wycherley's jaw drop open when Andrew Owens stepped timidly into the room. His hands shook uncontrollably and he stared at the floor. For once, he did not remove his hat out of respect.

"Mr. Owens has admitted to the crime that he and the other two men you enlisted committed upon your command," Sean announced.

Wycherley shrugged. "It is only one man's word against another."

Sean nodded to Andrew, and the young man eagerly turned and

disappeared from the room. "Mr. Owens has confessed to his sins in the presence of many witnesses," Sean explained, "I doubt that you will have many supporters in the community if you decide to oppose him. Besides, the Roberts boy is regaining his strength every day. Soon he will be well enough to tell us what happened in the woods."

Wycherley was careful not to respond.

"It is a pity that Adolphustown's quarterly court session was already held last month," Sean reminded Wycherley, "But there will be another in Kingston this fall, and this time, instead of appearing as a magistrate, you may very well be one of those on trial."

Wycherley rose up from his chair and banged a fist on his desk. "You do not know me well if you think I will stand for this, Brody," he growled.

The clamor from the crowd outside could be heard louder for a moment as the front door opened, "Everything is here!" Will called out from the hallway, then closed the door again, bringing silence back to the room.

"The land has been returned to its rightful owners," Sean told Wycherley, "I am sure your money was on Ryan and so you must have lost heavily on the fight today. There is little left here for you. I'd suggest you go back to the United States, Mr. Wycherley, or stay here and face prosecution for your many crimes."

"Do you really think that your threats are any match for Sheriff Cain's pistol, Reverend? Wycherley challenged.

"I imagine that his pistol has already been confiscated by the armed men we had waiting in the hallway," Sean answered confidently. "A message has already been dispatched to Kingston, and with the word of so many against you and Sheriff Cain, there is little chance that you will hold on to your position as an upholder of law and justice in the Fourth. In fact, you will be lucky if you aren't imprisoned immediately."

"You think you can stand in my study and talk that way to me?" Wycherley snarled, pointing a finger at Sean.

"Yes he can, and so can I!" a voice called out from the hallway, and a tall distinguished-looking white-haired man stepped into the room. Well-dressed in a dark jacket and matching trousers, he carried himself with an air of importance, and this was not lost on the house maid. Lucy followed timidly behind, blurting out an explanation to the master of the house. "He insisted on seein' you, Judge Wycherley! There are so many men in the hallway, I can't do nothin' to stop anyone!"

"Away with you then!" Wycherley barked, and she turned and hurried off.

"Judge Markham," Wycherley nodded, beads of sweat appearing on his forehead, "It is good to see you."

"Do not pretend, Franklin," Markham shot back, "I've heard everything. I'd had my suspicions about you for some time, but these are grave accusations against you. Attempted murder? Illegal land dealings? Not to mention staging a boxing match and establishing a betting post. Really, Franklin. Did you think the Courts would not discover your deception?"

"Everything was done by the letter of the law," Wycherley insisted.

"Then stay and defend yourself, or leave as Reverend Brody has suggested and hope that your troubles do not follow you," Judge Markham nodded, "But I believe there is reason enough to order an investigation that will lead to a subsequent trial. If you stay."

Wycherley swiped a hand across his desk and sent books, quill pens and ink flying across the room. "I should have known better than to think that the people of this backward colonial outpost would ever recognize progress when they see it."

"Progress, Judge Wycherley," Sean replied, "Means something different to the people of Adolphustown than it does to you."

*****

It was a particularly pleasant morning, and Willem and Sean were chopping wood near the cabin when two riders approached along the main path. As the horses drew nearer, Sean looked up, disbelief spreading across his face when he recognized the men. "Bishop Weston!" he exclaimed, planting his axe into the ground.

Willem was watching the riders now as well, and he raised a hand to wipe the sweat from his brow. Eliza, entertaining the younger children nearby, moved closer to hear what the visitors had to say.

The Bishop swept his long, dark cape away from his saddle and slowly dismounted.

"I hope you have journeyed well, Father!" Sean exclaimed.

"Why should a living man complain?" the Bishop replied, "It is true, I grow weak and old, but I am divinely assisted. And Reverend Beckett agreed to accompany me this far owing to the fact that he is to assist you in services this Sunday."

Sean nodded to Ezra and, smiling, turned to introduce Willem and Eliza to the newcomer. "Mr. and Mrs. Hollister, please meet the Bishop Arthur Weston and my good brother, Reverend Ezra Beckett," Sean paused before adding, "I must admit that your arrival here does come as some surprise, Father."

"For both of us, Reverend Brody," the Bishop nodded, "I would now in fact be resting quite comfortably in New York, were it not for some disturbing news that has come to my attention through of all people, an Anglican missionary from Bath."

A frown crossed Sean's face. "Josiah Hamm. He knows little of my work here, Father."

"I do think we should retire to a more private location to discuss our business," Bishop Weston suggested, glancing around as Charlotte stepped in beside Eliza and more onlookers began to gather.

"Better for the people to hear it directly from the source, Bishop," Sean advised, "Whatever you say to me today will eventually make the rounds anyway."

"That might explain how word reached the conference so quickly," Bishop Weston nodded.

"It's fortunate for Josiah Hamm that his correspondence moves far more quickly than he does," Ezra Beckett half-chuckled, then stifled his amusement when the Bishop shot him an unhappy glance.

"Ahh, now I see," Sean nodded, "Reverend Hamm felt it necessary to interfere in the business of our Methodist brethren."

Bishop Weston ignored the inference and got right to the point. "Reverend Brody, how do you respond to accusations that you have not lived up to your duties as Superintendent of the Bay of Quinte Circuit since your arrival?"

Sean looked surprised. "I have concentrated on nothing but my duties, Bishop. And I am disappointed that you would take the word of Reverend Hamm over mine."

"So there is no truth to the matter of your publicly swimming with kites?" Bishop Weston wondered.

Sean glanced at Charlotte, then back to the Bishop. "Father, with respect, I must inquire what sin there could be in cleansing one's own body?"

"Is it true that your daughter almost died while attempting to follow your foolish example?" the Bishop pressed.

"The girl is fine!" Willem jumped in, "Look!" and he pointed toward Abigail, who ran forward and curtsied.

Bishop Weston thought about this for a moment, then added, "And as to the charge of scuffling with natives?"

"I was merely defending myself, Father! The man insisted that I purchase a dress!" Sean insisted.

There were scattered chuckles from those around them, but the Bishop did not appear to be impressed. "Reverend Brody, may I remind you of the preacher's rules of conduct, which stipulate that you must avoid all lightness, jesting, and foolish talk?"

"And be ashamed of nothing but sin, Father," Sean added, "Let us not omit that rule of conduct, for I assure you that I have nothing of which to be ashamed."

Bishop Weston glanced around the settlement, slowly taking in the crowd of curious onlookers. "Tell me, Reverend Brody, why is it that I have come upon you chopping wood when you could be reading scriptures?"

"I read the scriptures daily between four and five a.m., Father, and again from five to six p.m.! My wife can attest to this." Sean pointed toward Charlotte and she nodded her agreement, "It's true, Father Weston."

The Bishop looked off toward the tavern, stared at it for a moment, then turned back to his riveted audience. "A Methodist preacher of your talents must preach the most where there are the greatest number of quiet and willing hearers, Reverend Brody."

Sean raised his voice a little, increasingly frustrated. "I gather you think that my talents are wasted here, Father Weston?"

"This tavern makes it quite clear to me that when all the seed has fallen by the wayside, there is scarce any fruit remaining in this settlement," the Bishop commented, "We can make better progress elsewhere, Reverend Brody. Missionaries are needed in Nova

Scotia."

Charlotte gasped and stepped forward, "These are good people, Bishop!" she protested, "We cannot desert them! They need Sean here!"

The Bishop appeared to ignore her plea and started back toward his horse.

"We know no one in Nova Scotia!" Charlotte called after him, desperate, "This is our home now!"

Bishop Weston did not turn back to her, but stopped before reaching his horse and said, "I will arrange a new posting for you, Mr. Brody. Oh, I mustn't forget. I have this for Mr. Hollister." He reached into the pocket of his cape, turning back to Willem with a bag of coins in his hand. "Your stipend," he offered.

Willem's face went red, though Sean wasn't sure if it was out of embarrassment or anger. The answer became clear when Willem reached down and grabbed his axe, gripping it tightly. Bishop Weston stepped back in apprehension and Ezra Beckett moved forward protectively, though both men soon saw that there was no need for any fear when Willem turned, axe in hand, and marched through the crowd toward the tavern. The settlers fell back to give him room, watching as Willem threw the axe high into the air and brought it down hard in the middle of the tavern sign. Then again. And again. Picking up the wooden pieces, he marched back over to the Bishop and dropped them on the ground in front of him.

"There's your fruit," Willem told him, "And keep your miserable stipend. I will not accept payment in exchange for allowing the word of God into my heart."

Bishop Weston glanced down at the shattered sign, thought for a moment, and then tucked the coin bag back into his pocket. Beckett helped him mount his horse and then he glanced down at Sean. "Oh by the way, Brother Lockwood's conscience overtook him recently. He admitted that you did not strike that man, or any man on the boxing stage in New York, though how you managed to fight without fighting will remain one of God's great mysteries," he finished. Charlotte grinned.

"You have my apologies for sending you off as I did without knowing the truth," Weston continued, "Though I must admit it does seem to have been for the best. Hope grows in the most unexpected places, Reverend Brody," he marvelled, "You may stay on in Adolphustown. Brother Beckett will report back to me with your progress. Good day to you all."

With that, Bishop Weston directed his horse back onto the path, and he and Beckett slowly disappeared into the forest.

*****

It was a hot August day when Ezra Beckett stepped in beside Sean, nodding to encourage him. Sean looked out at the tiny congregation, mainly comprised of Willem and Eliza Hollister and their children, the Van Horn family, a few scattered settlers, and a half dozen Mohawks. He took a deep breath, glanced briefly at his notes, and then began.

"Friends...welcome. I am the Reverend Sean Brody, and this is my assistant, the Reverend Ezra Beckett. How joyful that we can gather together in this--"

"This is blasphemy!"

The startled congregation turned to see Josiah Hamm standing in the doorway.

"This is my flock!" Hamm shouted, waddling forward along the aisle toward the lectern. "I am missionary to the Mohawks of Tyendinaga! Get up, people! Get up, get in your canoes, and make haste back to our meeting place across the bay! There is still time for God to forgive you this sin!"

A few of the natives seemed concerned and rose slowly from their seats. Degan stood and glanced down at Caroline, who was seated beside him with their baby son nestled, sleeping, in her arms.

"Stop!" Sean protested, addressing the congregation, "Wait! You have every right to follow whatever path you choose, but please consider that some tired paths end where new ones begin."

Degan stepped forward and stood with Sean and Hamm, addressing them both as he spoke. "I have listened closely to each of you over these past many weeks. Mr. Hamm, you have told me that there are two ways to go when we die, the bad way, and the good way."

"That is the truth, Mr. Hawke," Hamm nodded, staring smugly at Sean.

Degan continued. "You say that all drunkards, all wicked white men and all wicked Indians will go the bad way, and that good white people will go the good way."

"Indians may also go the good way if they become good and serve the Lord," Hamm added.

"But I do not want to go the white man's way," Degan shook his head, "My parents taught me that when we die, we all shall go where the sun sets, and I believe that this is where I will go. My wife, my son, they will choose where they want to go, but in the end, we all will be together."

"That is heresy!" Hamm shouted.

"It is what I believe," Degan announced, "It is what we believe," and he swept an arm out around him to include his fellow Mohawks, who nodded their agreement.

Hamm let out a huge sigh, then eyed Sean suspiciously. "Mr. Brody, do you honestly believe that you can convince these natives to stay, when even the residents of Adolphustown themselves have cast you off as the heretic that you are?"

"Only heretic in here is you, Mr. Hamm," Hugh Butler spoke up from the doorway, his powerful voice filling the church.

Sean looked toward the back of the church, amazed. The Butler family had arrived with six children in tow, even little Charlie, who was only two, happily chattering away in his older sister Margaret's protective arms.

"Please come in!" Sean welcomed them, "Mr. Butler, I have been told that you have done your share of preaching in this church when there was need in the past."

Hugh nodded his blonde head and smiled, approaching to shake Sean's hand. Charlotte rose from her bench and met Annabelle Butler halfway along the aisle.

"I hadn't prayed for a very long time until I saw the Roberts boy so near to death," Annabelle admitted, "I prayed for him. I prayed for you when your Abigail nearly drowned. But I'd rather pray in here with you today, if that's alright."

"Mrs. Butler, we would be honoured to have you and your family join us," Charlotte smiled, indicating an empty bench.

"Another family converted, Mr. Brody," Hamm chuckled, "At this rate you'll have this church full in, oh, seven or eight years!"

"It might be sooner than that, Reverend Hamm," Abraham Thurlow chimed in, and the growing congregation turned to see

Nettie and the entire Thurlow family filing in behind Abraham.

"There's more coming," Abraham assured Sean, removing his hat.

Charlotte turned toward Sean and beamed.

"Mr. Hamm, I would like to welcome you to the Hay Bay Methodist Church," Sean grinned, relaxing.

Hamm did not tarry long after this, turning to scoff at the group, then storming out past the cluster of people just entering.

"There'll be room enough for all," Sean shouted happily, "Come in! Come in!"

It was a joyous day thanks to a community finally rejoined in fellowship, free of the chains that had been imposed on their hearts and lives.

"I have very much enjoyed sharing this time with each of you this morning," Sean nodded as he finished the service, "And so that we may plan for next Sunday, I would ask that all who wish to hear any more such preaching to please rise up and show your intention to be here."

Charlotte and Abigail were the first to jump to their feet, followed by Eliza and Emma, along with Willem and the rest of the congregation until every man, woman and child was standing.

Charlotte could see that Sean was very pleased, and he swallowed hard before continuing. "Well then, please be seated as I remind you to expect preaching here again on Sunday next, at which time I understand Mrs. Hollister has offered to begin a Sunday school for the children."

Eliza nodded, smiling.

"We also congratulate Mr. Hollister on his newest undertaking, a general store, to be established on the site of his former tavern," Sean continued, and he glanced at Will, nodding from his seat.

"Adolphustown is a good place," Sean announced, "With many good things ahead for all of us."

"Is one of those good things our baby, Papa?" Abigail chimed in, and the congregation erupted in laughter.

"Yes, Little Abigail," Sean smiled, a lump forming in his throat, "Our baby." He glanced lovingly at his sweet Charlotte and added, "Just one of the many good things ahead for all of us here in the Fourth."

ABOUT THE AUTHOR

Rebecca Wilkinson's radio career keeps her busy through the week, but in her spare time she pursues her writing hobby with reckless abandon. Her screenplay "Discovering Emma" was produced as a low-budget feature film; she's been published in "Island Living" and "Dreamwest" magazines, and her e-book "To Love a Redcoat" is the sweeping tale of two star-crossed lovers from opposing sides who meet in Boston on the eve of the American Revolution. Rebecca lives in Napanee, Ontario with her two sons Zander and Carter, and will forever be thankful to her mother, writer Edna Wilkinson, for passing along the writing bug.

Manufactured by Amazon.ca
Bolton, ON

13365985R00092